What Teachers Can Learn From Sports Coaches

A Playbook of Instructional Strategies

Nathan Barber

 Routledge
Taylor & Francis Group

NEW YORK AND LONDON

First published 2015
by Routledge
711 Third Avenue, New York, NY 10017

and by Routledge
2 Park Square, Milton Park, Abingdon, Oxon OX14 4RN

Routledge is an imprint of the Taylor & Francis Group, an informa business

Library of Congress Cataloging-in-Publication Data

Barber, Nathan, 1971–
    What teachers can learn from sports coaches : a playbook of instructional strategies / Nathan Barber.
        pages cm
    1. Teaching.   2. Coaching (Athletics)   I. Title.
    LB1025.3.B3527 2014
    370.102—dc23
    2014005949

ISBN: 978-0-415-73826-2 (hbk)
ISBN: 978-0-415-73827-9 (pbk)
ISBN: 978-1-315-81750-7 (ebk)

Typeset in Palatino
by Apex CoVantage, LLC

CONTENTS

FOREWORD BY ANNETTE BREAUX

What's the difference between a great coach and a great teacher? In this book, Nathan Barber actually proves just how difficult it is to answer that question because the lines are quite blurred.

Great teachers – all of them, regardless of the ages of their students or the subject they teach – know how to inspire students. They know that before you can teach students anything, you have to help them to "want" what you are teaching. Great coaches inspire their players to "want" to perform at peak levels. Great coaches and teachers? No difference there.

For students, wanting something is not enough on the path to actually having something. Now they have to know "how" to get it. Because great teachers are great communicators, great teachers can make almost any task seem doable by their explanation and by their example. Great coaches can show players how to accomplish a difficult feat through quality instruction. Great coaches and teachers: what's the difference?

Both great coaches and teachers take people where they cannot go on their own. They provide careful, thoughtful instruction and guidance; they keep their eyes trained on the "ball" – not the physical ball, but rather the process of teaching – fostering creativity, deep thinking, problem solving, and collaboration; they build perseverance, determination, and resilience in their students and players. Most importantly, through example and by providing rich experiences, great coaches and teachers teach life lessons! In the hands of great coaches and teachers, everyone wins, regardless of the numbers on the scoreboard or the grade on the report card!

So what's the difference between great coaches and great teachers? In this compelling book, Nathan Barber proves that you can't be one without being the other!

Annette Breaux is an internationally known author, educational consultant, and speaker. Her previous books include *The Ten-Minute Inservice*, *Seven Simple Secrets*, and the national bestseller *101 Answers for New Teachers and Their Mentors*.

FOREWORD BY KIM MULKEY

I've been around the game of basketball my entire life. I've been blessed to enjoy incredible success as a player, as an assistant coach, and most recently as a head coach. As I reflect on my career, I think the common denominators of my basketball success have been a combination of hard work and time spent with great coaches. Much of what I do as a coach I learned from Leon Barmore at Louisiana Tech and Pat Summitt in the Olympics. Coach Summitt and Coach Barmore are both unbelievable leaders. They demand the utmost. Both make you exert yourself beyond what you think you are capable of giving. The way they coached and taught me have made an impact on how I coach my players today. My players know that I'm trying to make them better players and teach them how to play hard. I am motivated by challenge and an "I'll-show-you" mentality, and my hope is that this will motivate my players as well – the challenge to be the best they can be. In truth, it is about winning when you become a coach; almost nothing beats cutting down a net after winning a national championship or feeling the weight of an Olympic gold medal around your neck. But it's also about teaching life lessons.

In my autobiography, *Won't Back Down*, my dear friend and mentor Pat Summitt says about me, "she can teach and motivate young people" and "Those that get a chance to play for her will be better equipped to handle the real world when they leave Baylor, with the degree they earned in the classroom and the life lessons they learned on the basketball court." As much as I hope I've taught young women about the game of basketball, I hope I've taught them even more about life, about the value of hard work, and about the importance of getting a good education. I've always expected my players to be in class every day, no exceptions. I know the impact that great teachers can have, so I expect my players to reap the benefits of being exposed to great teaching.

Great teaching and great teachers are priceless, and I think the world undervalues our teachers today. Plain and simple, great teaching is hard work, whether that's on the basketball court or in the classroom. Finding new ways to motivate and challenge kids, staying on top of the latest techniques, and remaining at the top of your game at all times is challenging, difficult work. Some of the best, hardest-working teachers I know teach subjects like math and science, and others teach basketball, softball, and other sports. There's a great deal to be learned from these teachers, regardless of the content they teach.

Without a doubt, we all can benefit from the wisdom and experience of those who excel in their fields. With this book, Nathan Barber draws on the wisdom and experience of some of the best teachers in sports and translates that wisdom into best practices for your classroom. After all, great coaching involves great teaching and great coaches are great teachers. With hard work and a commitment to helping kids improve their lives, the lessons he's borrowed from the sports world can help you better challenge your students to be the best they can be and better equip them to handle the real world when they leave your classroom.

Kim Mulkey, a 2000 inductee into the Women's Basketball Hall of Fame, is the only player to win NCAA national championships as a player (Louisiana Tech, 1981 and 1982), as an assistant coach (Louisiana Tech, 1988), and as a head coach (Baylor University, 2005 and 2012). She also led her team to a gold medal in the 1984 Olympics.

ACKNOWLEDGMENTS

Many thanks to Routledge/Eye On Education, and specifically Lauren Davis, for believing in this project and its potential impact on teachers and teaching.

To Annette Breaux and Kim Mulkey, great teachers in your own right, for writing the forewords, I can't thank you enough. Each in your own way, you inspire me.

Thanks to Matt Shelton for tirelessly responding to scores of texts, calls, and email.

I'm afraid I'll never be able to express my gratitude sufficiently to the amazing coaches named below. As if the grind of coaching doesn't already consume their time, each coach below shared with me not only his or her precious time but also wisdom. I am indebted to each and am a better teacher now as a result of being challenged by the volumes of sage advice, insight, and teaching philosophy I've collected from these fine educators.

Bret Almazan-Cezar, Archbishop Mitty High School, women's volleyball

Leta Andrews, Granbury High School, women's basketball

Brian Boland, University of Virginia, men's tennis

Brian Brewer, Marietta College, baseball

Cori Close, UCLA, women's basketball

John Cohen, Mississippi State University, baseball

Anson Dorrance, University of North Carolina, women's soccer

Marv Dunphy, Pepperdine University, men's volleyball

Kurt Earl, Lincoln Christian School, football

Sean Fleming, Canada Soccer, U-17 men's national team

Brad Frost, University of Minnesota, women's ice hockey

Patti Gerckens, UC San Diego, softball

Kenny Guillot, Louisiana, retired, football

Mick Haley, USC, women's volleyball

Jeff Holman, Haddonfield Memorial High School, men's and women's tennis

Clint Hormann, Cedar Park High School, football

Hugh Marr, England Golf, boys' national team

Terry Michler, Christian Brothers High School, men's soccer

Dale Monsey, Texas, retired, men's basketball

Tom O'Grady, Team FLC, men's and women's lacrosse

Terry Schroeder, Pepperdine University, men's water polo

Brandon Slay, USA Wrestling, freestyle wrestling

Justin Spring, University of Illinois, men's gymnastics

Heather Tarr, University of Washington, softball

Tom Wilson, Dowling Catholic High School, football

M.L. Woodruff, Louisiana, retired, baseball

Kurt Zimmerman, Dowling Catholic High School, football

MEET THE AUTHOR

Nathan Barber has spent the last twenty years immersed in education. During that time, he has served his students as a teacher, coach, department chair, and administrator. As a classroom teacher, he taught a wide variety of social studies courses at both the middle and high school levels. His favorite courses included world history, European history, and historical films. His specialty in the classroom, AP European History, eventually opened the door for him to write books and online content for a number of publishers and test-prep companies. In addition to test-prep books and content specifically for AP European History students, Nathan's writing includes test-prep books for the GED and other standardized tests, classroom guides for teachers, and educational books covering such topics as US history and vocabulary.

For a decade, Nathan spent countless hours coaching high school basketball while teaching social studies. During that time, he prided himself on working diligently to excel not only on the court but also in the classroom. It was during his years of coaching and teaching that he began to make concrete connections between good teaching in the world of sports and in the classroom. To improve his teaching in both areas, he read voraciously, sought out mentors, and observed others frequently.

Nathan's experiences as both coach and teacher led him into school administration, a field he values because he can impact not only students but also the faculty who teach them. He currently serves as a high school principal in Houston. His faculty, peers, and colleagues recognize him as a creative, innovative, forward-thinking educator who seeks to challenge the status quo at every turn. Furthermore, he is recognized as an educational leader who values great teaching above all else.

Author of more than a dozen books, Nathan's other titles include *Master the AP European History Test*, *AP European History Success*, *The Complete Idiot's Guide to European History*, *Test-Prep Your IQ with the*

Essentials of Sports, and most recently a novel, *Resurrecting Lazarus, Texas*. Nathan spends his time in Texas coaching and challenging his faculty and students, investing in his family, writing, and managing his online presence, which includes Facebook, Twitter, and his blog, The Next Generation of Educational Leadership.

INTRODUCTION

What is a coach? The word *coach* seems to have originated in Hungary at some point in the sixteenth century and described a large carriage used for transportation. In the early nineteenth century, *coach* became an Oxford University slang term for a tutor who "carried" a student, as in preparation for university exams. Later in the nineteenth century, *coach* at last appeared in the vocabulary of sports as one who leads a team. An interesting thread runs through these three examples of *coach*. Do you see it yet?

We can deduce that *coach* morphed into the verb *coaching* at some point during the nineteenth century once the associations with tutoring and leading sports teams became commonplace. Now, in the twenty-first century, what lies at the heart of coaching actually can be traced back to its three original, unique, yet related uses. The all-time winningest high school men's soccer coach in the United States, *Terry Michler*, makes an astute observation about coaching in the modern world. Michler, who coaches at Christian Brothers College High School in St. Louis, Missouri, says, "[coaching] involves taking someone where they could not get on their own." With one short phrase, Michler sums up and ties together the three original applications of the word *coach*. All three of the original meanings of *coach* involved taking someone – a passenger, a student, an athlete – somewhere he or she couldn't go on their own – a distant geographic destination, the Dean's List, the league championship. A good coach does the same today.

Coaching is teaching. Who knows who first said this, but this phrase has been quoted and requoted countless times, and with good reason. A great coach also is a great teacher, even if the subject matter is zone defense, the pick and roll, the bunt, or the art of putting. Don't take my word for it, though. Consider what these great coaches have to say on the subject:

"The coach is first of all a teacher."

—John Wooden

"They are about as parallel as anything can be."

—*Terry Michler*

"At the end of the day, coaching is teaching."

—*Brian Boland*

"Coaching is teaching. Great coaches/teachers are good communicators; start with the end in mind; stress the fundamental (little things) concepts; practice and build on those fundamental concepts daily; reteach until the concept is mastered; motivate their students; and establish positive relationships with their students."

—*Dale Monsey*

"Coaching and teaching are one in the same in that the educator has one purpose in mind: to share knowledge with the student/athlete in the hopes of making them smarter both mentally and physically."

—*Patti Gerckens*

"Coaching obviously is synonymous with teaching because I think great coaching *is* effective teaching. What you're trying to do is to accelerate someone's growth in the game that you're an expert in, and you're trying to give them the benefit of your experience by sharing with them what they can do to get to their potential."

—*Anson Dorrance*

Even when the subject matter differs, great coaches and great teachers have a great deal in common. Great coaches and teachers communicate effectively, harness the power of teamwork, make work meaningful, embrace technology, build a winning tradition, teach life lessons, and seek continuous improvement. Drawing on the wisdom of some of the best and most successful coaches in the business today, this book draws parallels between great coaches and great teachers, between great coaching and great teaching. Using examples from the lives and experiences of these great coaches, this book illustrates the correlation between teaching in the sports world and teaching in the classroom. As you read through the book, note that coaches whose names are *italicized* have provided direct input for this book. Without their wisdom, this book would not have come together as such a practical yet meaningful guide to great teaching.

Although this book could be read cover to cover in a few sittings, each section has been divided into short, easily digestible pieces to be read and pondered and then applied. Additionally, because of the way the book has been structured, reading through the sections in order is not necessary. Browse the sections, find what interests you or what you need, then read, consider, and repeat. Regardless of how you read through the book, my hope is that you are challenged by the ideas presented here and that you find many of these ideas relevant and useful in your own teaching journey.

—Nathan Barber

Section I

Communicate Effectively

1

Communication is a Two-Way Street

> **"**Communication is huge! You must be able to communicate in a way that the players can understand on their terms. It also is important to be a good listener and observer.**"**
>
> *(Terry Michler*, all-time winningest high school soccer coach)

Coaches and teachers alike, especially those who are young or inexperienced, often feel compelled to dispense large volumes of valuable information, facts, data, strategies, procedures, and more, because they believe that's what's necessary to put players and students in a position to be successful. It can be tempting as a coach to stand and deliver hard-hitting speeches, pep talks, pre-game strategy, instruction about proper technique, or other coach-speak every time an opportunity presents itself for the coach to address the team. In this coaching model, if the coach is responsible for his players' development, the coach should transfer every ounce of knowledge from his brain to the players' brains to maximize their growth, and he should do so as often as possible. Likewise, when this model is used in the classroom, it's common for the teacher to wax poetic about the US Constitution, absolute value, dinosaurs, tone and voice, or whatever the topic, for every minute of every class period. In this teaching model, if the teacher is responsible for students' learning, the teacher should be the source of a one-way flow of information because the students need to hear everything the teacher has to say (and the teacher usually has *a lot* to say).

Effective coaches and teachers immediately will recognize these models as coach-centered and teacher-centered, rather than student-centered, and as generally ineffective and obsolete. So why do some coaches and teachers believe it's their primary responsibility to be the sole source of useful information? Probably because that's the coaching or teaching model they were exposed to as a student, player, student teacher or assistant coach, and because they believe communication is a one-way street.

Coach Tony DiCicco, head coach of the US women's national soccer team during its 1996 gold-medal run through the Olympic Games, devotes an entire chapter of his book *Catch Them Being Good* to the art of communication. DiCicco states early in the chapter, "The first thing you have to learn about communication is how to listen and observe." In other words, communication involves more than a one-way flow of information. Information must flow in two directions, both to and from the coach, and that will happen only when a coach combines instruction with listening and observation. Practically speaking, communication must be a two-way street.

A coach has great instructional information to give his players. Players need to hear what their coach has to say about their strengths and weaknesses, how to improve, and how to prepare for the next match. Players need to hear their coach's vision and expectations. If the coach is the only one speaking, though, or if speaking is the only thing a coach does, there is no two-way street. The same can be said of the teacher in the classroom. The teacher possesses much information the students need in order to learn, to grow, and to be successful. If the teacher is the only person in the classroom speaking, or if lecturing is the only thing a teacher does, there's little to no communication.

Countless opportunities arise during the season for any coach to provide instruction and guidance for his players – during practice, in classroom sessions, pre-game, during timeouts, at halftime, after the game, at the next practice. The effective coach, though, takes advantage of opportunities for communication as described by DiCicco, opportunities to listen and observe. The effective coach listens carefully to what his players say and how they say it. He listens to the questions they ask as well as to their answers to his questions, all the while looking for clues that can direct his feedback. He observes his players, watching their body language, their execution of drills or plays, all the while looking for evidence of their understanding.

Any teacher has the opportunity to provide direct instruction from bell to bell every day. Direct instruction does not meet DiCicco's standard of communication, though. The effective teacher, like the effective coach, seizes opportunities to really communicate by listening to students' questions and answers, as well as to conversation between students during collaboration. The effective teacher also observes students' body language, seeking clues as to their confidence, frustration, or confusion. Using the information gleaned from listening and observing, like the effective coach, the teacher can effectively direct the appropriate feedback to the students.

The most meaningful teaching and learning occurs when coaches and players, as well as teachers and students, stay the course on the two-way street of communication. Coaches and teachers alike must keep open the lines of communication, listen to what players and students have to say, and watch for nonverbal cues that can direct future teaching. The better a coach or teacher listens and observes, the better the quality of appropriate instruction and feedback he can provide. The better the instruction and feedback, the more equipped the players or students will be for growth and success.

2

Plan for Success

❝I deeply believed that the teacher and coach who
has the ability to properly plan . . . from both
the daily and the long-range point of view
together with the ability to devise the necessary
drills to meet his particular needs
for maximum efficiency, has
tremendously increased his possibility of success.❞

(John Wooden, legendary men's basketball coach at UCLA,
coach of ten NCAA national championship teams)

"Failure to plan is to plan for failure." Various versions of this quote have floated about now for decades, with one iteration attributed to Benjamin Franklin, one to Winston Churchill, and another to Alan Lakein. Regardless of who first offered this sage advice, the phrase rings true on many levels for both coaches and teachers. Without a doubt, coaches and teachers who fail to develop game plans and lesson plans will come up short more often than not. Coaches and teachers need to plan for many aspects of their daily interactions with students and players, but perhaps no facet of their daily interactions requires more planning than communication.

When coaches speak to teams and players without being strategic about what they're going to say – be it in practice, in a game, in the locker room, or after a game – the result can be unfortunate. How many coaches have launched into an off-the-cuff diatribe without thinking about the words spewing forth? Probably many, if not most. If we could ask those coaches how effective those sessions were, most of the respondents likely would request do-overs because of the ineffectiveness of what and how they communicated. Great coaches, because they are great communicators, spend considerable time planning not only drills and exercises, game plans, and last-minute plays, but also pre-game, halftime, and post-game addresses, one-on-one conversations, teaching sessions, and more.

Whether in the arena or in the classroom, the most effective communications between teacher and student have been well-planned. *Brandon Slay*, Olympic gold medalist in the 2000 Olympic Games and current USA Wrestling freestyle coach, knows more than a little about thinking ahead about what to say to those he teaches. Slay says, "I plan out what I want to say often before I say it. For example, before practice starts in the afternoon, I'll think about what my intro is to practice. I may come up with a good quote, an illustration, or story to encourage them that day. For my communication to be effective, I plan it out in advance. I think it helps that when I get there I've already thought it out, visualized it." For Slay, planning ahead goes far beyond being organized and thoughtful. Says Slay about planning his communication with his wrestlers, "When I start communicating with them, it comes out more powerfully, passionately."

To be a great teacher, one must be a great communicator. Therefore, a great teacher who wants to maximize every opportunity for communication follows Slay's example and plans ahead every time. The various ways a great teacher communicates daily, numerous indeed, require forethought and planning. From greeting her classes each day to motivating her students to providing direct instruction to speaking with parents, and more, a great teacher cannot afford ill-planned communications. This may seem obvious, but its importance cannot be overstated. The most effective instruction has been planned and thought out thoroughly. Students of all ages have the uncanny ability to sniff out disorganization, poor planning, and fly-by-the-seat-of-your-pants teaching. A great teacher expects her students to be organized and forward thinking, so she must model these traits in her daily approach to communication. Even a lesson that's been taught a hundred times can be added to or improved upon with some additional forethought. Using Slay's advice, a great teacher might want to spend some time thinking about a quote to incorporate or a story to add to make things more interesting or to drive home a point. Additionally, as Slay contends, when communication has been planned thoughtfully, the communication becomes more powerful and illustrates the great teacher's passion. This principle can be extended to other facets of a teacher's professional life, too. Communication with the principal or counselor, speaking to an assembly, team, or club, speaking on behalf of one's school, and even communication via the written word require forethought and planning to be most effective.

Careful planning adds value to the "what" that a teacher communicates. However, careful planning and forethought can empower a great teacher to improve the "how" of communication, too. Any teacher can address a class as if all students were of equal ability, as if all students learned the same way, and as if all students had the same needs. Only a great teacher, though, communicates in such a way that all students "get it" and feel as though the teacher's lesson has been intentionally designed with them in mind. Communication at this level requires great thought and careful consideration ahead of time, but it can be done. Such powerful communication also may require a great teacher to change the way she typically communicates or has communicated in the past. Without question, such strategic and intentional communications skills require time, patience, and hard work, and become more effective over time with lots of practice. When it happens, though, and light bulbs go on all over the room . . . what a great moment.

As Brandon Slay says of his own teaching with USA Wrestling: "When I speak to my athletes, I don't speak to them as if I were giving a speech to a group of people. I really try to speak to them as if I were sitting down with them one on one. I try to speak to the group as if I were speaking to one, so that way they each feel like I'm talking directly to him. A lot of them will say, 'Coach, I know you were speaking to the whole group, but it sure seemed like you were talking directly to me.'" In other words, Slay works very hard at not giving a speech or presentation to the group like now-obsolete stand-and-deliver instructors once did, but rather at truly connecting with each of his athletes. Even when he's addressing a group, his focus remains not on being the center of attention but on meeting the needs of each of his athletes through his communication. A great teacher in his own right, Slay will be the first to say that such effective communication on the wrestling mat or in the classroom requires hard work and, most importantly, careful planning ahead of time.

3

The Problem with Praise

❝The trouble with most of us is that we would
rather be ruined by praise than saved by criticism.**❞**

(Norman Vincent Peale)

The spoken word, when used either correctly or incorrectly, can change a young person's life for better or for worse. Anyone who has coached or taught at any level has observed the power of the spoken word. Negative, condescending, or sarcastic words tear players and students down, damage their self-esteem, and inflict emotional pain and suffering. On the other hand, positive words, words of praise, build up players and students. Or do they?

Researchers like Carol Dweck, Ph.D., a psychologist from Stanford University, have explored this very topic in recent years and have made some surprising discoveries. In particular, the results of Dweck's studies indicate that the wrong kind of praise actually harms young people, discourages them from taking risks, and teaches them that they are valued for characteristics rather than for effort. Dweck discovered that children learn to identify with labels they're given through praise and they avoid taking risks that may mess up their labels. Therefore, Dweck warns against making statements like "You're so smart," "You're so pretty," and even "Good job." When children hear phrases like this, their performance actually worsens and their effort decreases because they fall back on the intelligence, etc., for which they've been praised.

Dweck told ABC News in 2007, "Parents should praise their children for their effort, their concentration, their strategies." In other words, parents should offer encouragement that validates effort. Parents should encourage with statements like, "Your hard work and studying for that exam really paid off," or "All your practice prepared you well for that performance." These statements teach young people that they have the power to change and to improve.

Great coaches may or may not be aware of Dweck's research. They have, however, long understood Dweck's premise. A great coach knows that any affirmation given to players must be done in a way that validates effort and encourages future hard work. Otherwise, empty praise goes straight to players' heads! Imagine a golf coach high-fiving a player after a difficult, tournament-winning putt and saying, "You sure are talented." A great golf coach would say something like, "All those hours on the putting green have finally paid off." Imagine a football coach telling a quarterback, "You have a fantastic arm," instead of saying, "You read the defense perfectly and hit the receiver exactly as we practiced all week." Picture the reaction of a volleyball player if her coach said, "You jump so high," instead of, "All your work in the weight room has you out-jumping everyone else on the team and clearing the net by several inches more than last year." Finally, imagine a swimming coach telling a swimmer after a record-setting heat, "You're just better than everyone else in the pool," instead of, "The adjustments we made on your turns definitely have shaved seconds off your time." If coaches constantly tell their players how fast, strong, talented, and skilled they are, the players' effort will drop and so will their performance.

The caveat against praise applies equally to the classroom, and great teachers understand. A great teacher recognizes the importance of affirming effort, improvement, and growth. A great math teacher, for example, would tell his student, "Your extra study time really showed on those geometric proofs," instead of, "You're a brilliant mathematician." Only one of those phrases encourages the student to work hard the next time a challenge arises. Likewise, a great art teacher would say, "Because of your patience and attention to detail, your portrait is incredibly lifelike," instead of, "You have such natural, artistic ability." One of those phrases does nothing but encourage the student to rest on talent rather than strive for improvement. Imagine an English teacher telling a student, "You're a brilliant writer," instead of, "Your clever use of metaphors made me want to read your essay over and over." That student likely would not work as hard on the next writing assignment because the teacher failed to recognize the student's writing endeavors.

Another interesting problem arises when coaches and teachers praise rather than encourage and affirm. Empty praise such as, "You're so talented" and "You're so smart," creates a label for the player or student with which he will come to identify himself. Once a player or student identifies with the label given by a coach or teacher, he becomes risk averse. He often goes out of his way to avoid the possibility of appearing not talented or not smart. Furthermore, the first time the player is challenged by or loses to someone bigger, stronger, faster, or more skilled, he begins to question his talent. After all, his coach said he was talented, but after losing, he's no longer so sure about that. The same will happen with a student when he runs into a challenging problem, assignment, or project. If the challenge seems too great, or if he doesn't earn an outstanding grade, he begins to question his own intelligence. If he really is as smart as the teacher says, he'll think, this problem couldn't possibly present this much difficulty. Had the coach been affirming work ethic and skill development, and the teacher affirming effort, neither would begin to question their innate abilities. When the ultimate goal of both coaching and teaching is the empowerment of young people to change and improve their own lives, praising anything other than efforts to improve sends entirely the wrong message.

4

Being a Master Motivator

"Good teachers and good coaches motivate.
You can have the best message in the world, as
a teacher or a coach, but if it's not delivered in
a motivational way, the kids aren't going to get it.**"**

(*John Cohen*, baseball coach, Mississippi State University)

Some of the most meaningful words great coaches say actually have little or nothing to do with plays, positions, balls, offense, defense, or anything else specific to his or her sport. Some of the most meaningful, and memorable, things coaches say are words designed to motivate players, teams, and even other members of the coaching staff. In the sports world, a number of coaches have become famous for their motivational skills, and specifically for their motivational pre-game or halftime speeches. For example, Knute Rockne, the legendary Notre Dame football coach who won four national championships between 1918 and 1930, delivered one of the most famous halftime speeches ever during the halftime of the 1928 game against the Army Cadets. Rockne needed a way to motivate his Fighting Irish squad, which had battled to a 0–0 halftime tie with Army. In the locker room at halftime, Rockne told his team about George Gipp, a former Notre Dame football star who had played years earlier and who died of pneumonia in 1920. According to Rockne, George Gipp said on his deathbed that one day when the team was down he should tell the team to go out and win one for the Gipper. Whether Gipp ever said that, we'll never know, but Rockne got the results he wanted. Notre Dame secured the 12–6 win in the second half.

Another great motivator, Herb Brooks, motivated a special group of underdog hockey players just before a medal-round hockey game in the 1980 Olympics. Brooks motivated Team USA to play against the powerhouse Soviet team with this fiery speech, considered by many to be one of the greatest motivational speeches ever: "Great moments are born from great opportunity. And that's what you have here tonight, boys. That's what you've earned here tonight. One game. If we played 'em ten times, they might win nine. But not this game. Not tonight. Tonight we skate with 'em. Tonight we skate with 'em and we shut them down because we can! Tonight we are the greatest hockey team in the world. You were born to be hockey players – every one of ya. And you were meant to be here tonight. This is your time. Their time is done. It's over. I'm sick and tired of hearing about what a great hockey team the Soviets have. Screw 'em! This is your time!" Brooks' players responded in grand fashion and upset the heavy favorites 4–3. Team USA went on to defeat Finland in the next game and capture the Olympic gold medal.

Another great motivational speech comes from the annals of the NFL and the great Vince Lombardi, for whom the Super Bowl trophy is now named. This speech, even more than the other two great speeches referred to already, provides a great model for teachers. Before Super Bowl II in 1968, a game in which the Green Bay Packers had a chance to win back-to-back titles, Lombardi challenged his team with the following words: "Boys if I were you I would be so proud of that [the opportunity to win a second consecutive Super Bowl] I would just fill up. It's not going to come easy. This is a club [the Oakland Raiders] that's going to hit you and try and hit you. You are just going to take it out of them. Just hit, just run, just block, just tackle. You do that and there is no question what the answer is going to be in this ball game. Keep your poise. There is nothing that they can show you out there you haven't faced a number of times." Lombardi's approach proved to be spot-on, as the NFL's Packers defeated the AFL's Raiders by a score of 33–14.

Lombardi's speech offers a marvelous example for how a great teacher might motivate her students today. A great teacher, after all, offers as much motivation for her students as she does content information and instruction. In his Super Bowl II speech, Lombardi talks about pride and opportunity, two things a great teacher might mention in a motivational speech before a big exam in a course, before a college admissions standardized test like the SAT or ACT, or before a state assessment. Lombardi includes a somewhat emotional appeal, but the brilliance of his words lies in the fact that he reminded his players of the fundamentals he's taught and they've mastered – hitting, running, blocking, and tackling. His words express confidence, both in what he's taught and in what the players have learned, therefore instilling his players with confidence, just as a great teacher would with her class full of students. He even prompts his players on just how ready they are by reminding them that they won't encounter anything they haven't already seen a number of times, just like a great teacher would do with her students.

Pre-game and halftime provide great opportunities for coaches to make memorable statements when teams need some motivation. Moments before practices and before important plays – such as defensive stands or game-winning field goal attempts – also provide coaches with the chance to get a team excited or calm, to communicate an important reminder, or to make a plan for the big moment. Likewise, timeouts, visits to the mound in baseball, changes of possession, and various dead-ball moments in other sports provide shorter, often more private opportunities for coaches to motivate with powerful or profound words. Great coaches seize these opportunities to instill confidence in players, to fire players up or to calm them down, or to encourage them to do more than the players think they can do. Coaches who are great communicators, though, do not rely only on the high-pressure, big-stage moments to motivate players, and they don't always use long speeches. In fact, the very best communicators work daily to motivate players, and they do so in a number of ways. Great coaches encourage players with the spoken word, with motivational email or handwritten notes, with pats on the back (or backside!), or even with simple gestures like a smile or a thumbs up. Great coaches, because they know their players and their players' personalities and needs, try to motivate each player in precisely the way he needs to be motivated. Sometimes great coaches motivate in public, in front of other players, and sometimes coaches motivate privately so only the player or players he's addressing hear what's being communicated. Great coaches know when to be subtle or discreet and when to be loud or public.

The most meaningful and powerful words teachers say may have absolutely nothing to do with grammar, formulas, battles, dinosaurs, vocabulary, or any other academic subject. The most powerful words from a teacher may be words of motivation she provides her students. Like great coaches, great teachers have numerous opportunities to offer motivation. Those opportunities may arise before a big exam, at the beginning of the semester or school year, before a class, or right in the middle of a lesson on a challenging concept. However, great teachers also work daily to communicate a positive message and to motivate their students. All students, not just those who struggle, need some motivation from teachers and not just before big exams. Great teachers know this and provide the necessary motivation to build confidence, to calm, to energize, to encourage, or to recognize progress, just as great coaches do. They motivate by speaking kind words, by writing encouraging notes on assignments, by sending inspiring notes or email, and by displaying quality work for all to see. Nonverbally, great teachers motivate students by patting them on the back, by being liberal with strategically timed smiles, by writing quotes on the board, by adding gold stars or stickers to papers, and myriad other ways. Great teachers, because they know their students, understand when students need motivation in public or in private, as well as what kind of motivation and how often. They know when to exercise discretion and when to let the whole world in on the motivation. Every player and every student needs a little pick-me-up now and then, and great coaches and teachers work hard to meet those needs not only on the big stage at pivotal moments but also in the routine of the day-to-day. Just as great coaches often are remembered as great motivators, so, too, are great teachers.

5

Communicate "Mastery," not "Performance"

> **"**Students with mastery orientation seek
> to improve their competence.
> Those with performance
> orientations seek to prove their competence.**"**
>
> (Gregory Schraw)

Perhaps more than any other question, coaches hear this one from players: "How can I get more playing time?" This especially is true for coaches in youth sports. With so much emphasis in the sports world on performance and statistics, can it be any wonder that players tend to ask coaches what can be done to earn more playing time, to move up the depth chart, or to earn a starting position on the team? Although these questions usually are well-intentioned, they indicate to a coach that the player has his priorities out of balance. Parents usually ask the same questions because they, too, often focus on the wrong things when considering their child's position on a team. In truth, a good coach can answer those questions for any parent or player at any time. A coach must be attentive to the strengths and weaknesses of players and should be able to present these to any player who asks about playing time or moving up the depth chart. However, a good coach knows that performance-based questions aren't the questions

17

the players need to ask, and a good coach knows how to redirect the player to ask the right questions.

When presented with questions about playing time, improving statistics, or receiving a starting position, a good coach redirects the player away from performance criteria and emphasizes improvement of particular skills or even mastery. The coach might even say, "You're asking the wrong question. Instead of asking how you can get more playing time, you need to be asking what areas of your game you most need to work on during practice and on your own time." It might be easy for a basketball coach to respond to a playing time question with, "To get more playing time, you need to be a better dribbler and you need to be a better shooter. To earn a starting position, you have to dribble and shoot better than the players already in the starting lineup." This answer, however, does not provide anything tangible or quantifiable for the player. When presented with such a question, a good basketball coach would respond to that player with something like, "I know you've improved your dribbling lately, but you're still very inconsistent dribbling with your left hand, especially against pressure. I can give you some drills to practice on your own that will help with left-handed dribbling. Additionally, your jump shot has been inconsistent beyond ten feet. I can work with you on shooting the mid-to-long range jumpshot if you can stay after practice. Once you've improved these two specific areas of your game, you may be skilled enough to compete for a starting position, but your focus needs to be on improving your skills."

Players often believe if they can just figure out what a coach is looking for then they can get more playing time or become a starter. Likewise parents often think coaches have some elusive formula for evaluating talent that dictates how playing time is divided amongst players. Such players and parents have missed the point entirely. A good coach constantly assesses and reassesses player development, then assigns playing time and positions based on players' mastery of skills. The more a player improves skills or the more a player moves toward mastery of a particular skill, the more likely that player is to be rewarded with more playing time or a more prestigious position. A good coach communicates this to both parents and players regularly and articulates his value of mastery over performance, of improvement and skill development over statistics.

Like their coaching counterparts, teachers often face a barrage of performance-centered questions from students and parents. "How can I do better on tests?" "How can I make an A?" "How can I move up in my class rank or standings?" "How do I figure out what you're looking for so I can make better grades?" Because years of schooling have conditioned students to think more about performance than mastery, such questions often are innocent and well-intentioned. After all, is it so wrong for a student to want to know how to improve her grade? A good teacher understands the nature of these questions but also knows how to refocus the student on what actually matters. A good teacher knows how to train students to ask the right questions, questions centered on mastery rather than on performance.

When meeting with a student, or her parents, a teacher might be presented with questions about earning a better grade in French class. The response easily could be, "If you want a better grade in French, you need to study harder for tests and spend more time on your homework assignments." A good teacher, though, would not answer this way because this response puts the student no closer to the goal of the course, which is moving the student closer to mastery of the French language. A good teacher might begin with a restatement of the question that reiterates what she's already communicated about mastery as opposed to performance. "You're asking the wrong question," she might say. "Instead of asking how to receive a better grade in French, you should be asking what areas of learning the French language need your attention most right now. Your long-term goal should be mastery of the French language, not an A. Your short-term goals should include mastery of both spelling and pronunciation of the days of the week and months of the year. Two other short-term goals for you need to be mastery of the weekly vocabulary lists and proper use of the accent marks. If you focus on your grade, you may never master the language. If you focus on mastering the language, on the other hand, your grade certainly will take care of itself."

Students, like athletes, sometimes believe they must figure out what a teacher is looking for in order to get that elusive A. They think there is some trick to getting an A, some mysterious thing the teacher wants to see or hear that must be the secret to better grades. Students under the direction of a good teacher know differently. Students blessed to receive coaching from a good teacher understand that hard work, adherence to the instructional plan laid out by the teacher, and focus on mastery necessarily will lead to better grades. Ideally, they also know that the goal of the course is learning and not making a grade. How will students know this? A good teacher, like a good coach, consistently emphasizes mastery over performance and demonstrates that learning and improvement far outweigh better grades or moving up in class standings. Additionally, when students and parents lose focus and ask questions about improving grades rather than asking questions about mastering content or improving skills, a good teacher redirects them and helps them ask the right questions.

6

Teaching and Reteaching
to Mastery

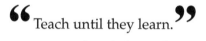

“Teach until they learn.**”**

(Leta Andrews, all-time
winningest high school
women's basketball coach)

Imagine for a moment that a coach introduces a new concept or skill to his team at practice. Imagine that coach moving quickly through the instruction, then moving on to something new or different regardless of the players' understanding. Imagine this happening not just once, but regularly. Fast forward a week, a month, to mid-season, to a time when the players need to draw on the knowledge the coach glossed over, or to a situation in which the players need a skill they never mastered. What might the win–loss record be for that team? What might the morale of the players be? How long will that coach last with that team? What kind of teacher is that coach? A great coach understands great teaching and simply would not allow this to happen.

After notching more than 500 wins at Axtell High School, a small school in Texas, former basketball coach *Dale Monsey* knows a thing or two about great teaching. One of the most important things to remember, says Monsey, is, "Great coaches and teachers reteach until a concept is mastered." His basketball players would have been hard-pressed to shoot a left-handed layup if they had not mastered dribbling left-handed. Likewise, had his players not learned to play solid man-to-man defense, they hardly could have been expected to use a man-to-man full court press effectively. Did all of his players master those skills the first time he introduced them? Monsey would be the first to say no, which is why checking for understanding and reteaching played such a pivotal role in the development of his players over the years.

Consider a swim coach whose team hasn't mastered turns, a soccer coach whose team hasn't mastered throw-ins, a baseball coach whose team hasn't mastered baserunning, or a volleyball coach whose team hasn't mastered setting. If a coach's responsibility is to take players where they cannot go on their own through solid teaching and reteaching, a coach has shirked his responsibility if he moves on to a new concept before a player or players have mastered the concept or skill at hand. After all, in sports as in the classroom, learning and skill mastery builds or scaffolds in progression. Skills and concepts taught early on will be necessary for mastery of new skills and concepts later. After teaching a new skill or concept, a great coach first checks to see if his players have mastered a concept, then reteaches until his players achieve mastery.

Players in all sports, just like students in classrooms, arrive to practice each at different places in his or her development, both cognitively and physically. When a coach introduces a new concept or skill, he has the responsibility to ensure all his players, not just the stars, have mastered the concept or skill. If there are players who do not understand, a great coach reteaches, and this is where a great coach distinguishes himself from everyone else. First, a great coach checks continuously for understanding. This can be done by observing players during guided practice or drills, looking specifically for clues that signal a lack of understanding. Likewise, as recommended by *Bret Almazan-Cezar*, coach of the seven-time California state volleyball champions Archbishop Mitty High School, a great coach who is "constantly checking for understanding" can have players "say it in their own words, or get them to give you a smile or a thumbs up when they understand." Second, when a great coach reteaches, he presents the concept or skill in a different way, using perhaps a different technique, different vocabulary, or even a different instructor. A great coach repeats this two-part cycle until all players have demonstrated mastery, and only then can he move on to something new.

Occasionally, one or two players struggle a little more than others on the team with certain skills or concepts. Tackling this challenge may require a little extra work on the part of the coach and the players. A common way great coaches handle such situations is through the use of stations, or particular areas on the field or court before, during, or after practice where players can work specifically on the problematic skill or concept, either with a coach or with other players. From Little Dribblers to NCAA athletic programs, stations provide great opportunities for coaches to reteach in a new or different way and work with their players toward mastery. Achieving mastery for all players on a team may require a player to spend extra time with a coach, but a great coach will not leave a player behind.

As great coaches do, great teachers introduce new information or concepts then constantly check for understanding to determine whether reteaching is necessary. When introducing new concepts in the classroom, a great teacher ties the new concept to information or ideas that the students have mastered already, and perhaps even explains how the new concept will be used in the future. An excellent way to introduce new information involves breaking the information down into small digestible bits, a method that educational guru Robert Marzano calls "chunking." Chunking the information can make both teaching and learning more efficient and can make checking for understanding more effective and timely.

When checking for understanding, great teachers assess their students much like great coaches do with their players. Just as Almazan-Cezar recommends for athletes, students in the classroom can give nonverbal cues like a thumbs up or a smile to indicate understanding, or they can raise their hand or give a thumbs down to indicate confusion. Great teachers not only can teach their students to use such cues but also can watch for more subtle nonverbal cues like a furrowed brow, crossed arms, or a frown. Assessments to check for understanding and mastery can be formal assessments like quizzes or assignments, or informal assessments like Q&A in the classroom. With the advent of educational technology, teachers can use electronic response devices commonly referred to as clickers to check students' understanding, too. Assessments are vital not only to show levels of student understanding but also to show a teacher which part of the concept she may need to reteach. Once a great teacher has checked for understanding, she can move on with the class to new concepts, or she can reteach if necessary. As Clint Hormann from Cedar Park High School says of teaching a concept, "If we do something during practice that is not done correctly, we do not move on to new material . . . We repeat that material until the athlete understands what he is supposed to do, and only then do we move on." This approach makes perfect sense for a great teacher in the classroom, too.

Great coaches and teachers alike have embraced the "teach and reteach" concept for generations. In the 1980s, Madeline Hunter formalized the concepts of checking for understanding, guided practice, and reteaching in her work on mastery teaching. In its most simple form, reteaching involves teaching concepts again when and if students do not understand. Great teachers practice this worldwide. Effective reteaching occurs either after a teacher has observed students struggling with a concept or after an assessment of some kind reveals gaps in student understanding. In the classroom as on the court or field, effective reteaching involves building on skills or information that's already been taught but teaching in a different way. Reteaching a concept in the same way it was taught the first time will yield the same results – incompetence, ineffectiveness, confusion, and low morale. A great teacher finds a new way to present the concept she's reteaching, using perhaps different terminology, a different perspective, different practice problems, or even a different teacher. A great teacher does not hesitate to ask a colleague or another student to explain things differently if one of her students still can't grasp a concept. Guiding a student through a concept he doesn't understand may take extra time – perhaps working one-on-one outside of class – but a great teacher will not leave a student behind.

7

The Tough Conversations

> ❝Most problems reach a resolution if parties are willing and able to communicate. The whole point of building honest and trustworthy relationships with your players is so that they feel comfortable communicating with their coach . . . Communication is everything.❞
>
> (*Brian Boland*, men's tennis coach at the University of Virginia, 2008 ITA National Coach of the Year, and 2013 NCAA national champion)

Every great coach desires success for each of his players on the field or court. A coach's dream would be for each of his players to develop his athletic skills and abilities to full potential, and to mature into a great individual and team player, at the same rate as every other player. Furthermore, a coach's dream would be for each player to ascend to the same high level of athletic skill and proficiency. Unfortunately, these are just dreams. All players have varying strengths and weaknesses, varying degrees of skill, varying rates of development, and varying ceilings for athletic accomplishment. Because of these variations, a great coach must address each player as an individual, must work with each player on his or her own development, and must provide feedback specific to that player. A great coach can't always address the team with feedback about progress and development and expect individuals to transfer that knowledge to their own skillset. The best individual growth occurs when a great coach works one-on-one with each player and provides feedback that specifically addresses each player's strengths and weakness, progress, and plan for continued improvement. Congratulating a player on growth and development can be great fun and presents very little challenge for most people. Most people love to offer encouragement and compliments. The tough part tends to be providing honest feedback when things aren't going so well, when a player is in a slump, when a player can't shake some bad habits, when a player continues to make the same mistake over and over, or when a player simply isn't working hard enough.

One of the most challenging tasks a coach faces with his players is having the tough conversations with players about their weaknesses and their growth areas. Even though great coaches know players need to hear such feedback, great coaches don't always enjoy these conversations. Simply put, most players don't like to hear or talk about their weaknesses and shortcomings, and they often perceive such feedback as negative or critical. These conversations have the potential to strain the coach–player relationship if they aren't handled carefully, yet these conversations must happen for players to grow, to fix mistakes, and to reach their potential. So how do great coaches approach such potentially touchy topics?

A great coach provides for each of his players an honest, objective perspective on each player's ability, strengths, and weaknesses. For this to be most effective, the player must perceive the feedback as non-threatening, encouraging, and supportive. Without a healthy relationship in place between coach and player, a player likely will never perceive the tough conversation in a positive way. A positive, healthy relationship between coach and player lays the foundation for all communication and makes possible those tough conversations.

Brad Frost took over the University of Minnesota women's ice hockey team in 2008 and in a matter of a few short years led the program to back-to-back NCAA national championships. This incredible success did not happen without open lines of communication and more than a few tough conversations between Frost and his players about what they needed to do to get better. Says Frost about the process, "Communication is one of the most critical things when leading people. It is also one of the hardest skills to master . . . You need to get to know your players so you can use an effective strategy when communicating with them one-on-one." Regarding his approach to handling tough conversations, Frost explains, "I try to be as direct as possible, even though it is tough sometimes." Pepperdine men's volleyball coach *Marv Dunphy*, who has five NCAA titles of his own, echoes Frost's direct, honest approach. He, too, prefers the one-to-one, individual method of working with each player so he can say, "Here is where you are improving, here's where you are, and here's where we need to go."

Another great coach who has navigated his share of tough conversations is *Justin Spring*, former Olympian and current men's gymnastics coach at the University of Illinois. The youngest coach in NCAA history to be named National Coach of the Year, Spring has led six gymnasts to individual NCAA titles and he guided Illinois to an NCAA team championship in 2012. Drawing on his experience as both an elite gymnast and as a coach of elite gymnasts, Spring offers a great, practical strategy for approaching the tough conversation. He says: "Always start off tough conversations with stating your intentions first. 'My intention for having this conversation is . . . (to help you achieve your goal of_____).' It is a great way to clear the space, or eliminate some of the baggage that people can bring into a meeting. The meaning of conversations can get lost very quickly, because everyone has their own unique filter of information. Cutting right to the core intention for having the conversation first, and then getting into details is a great way to align everyone's perception. I think we all can say we've had a conversation where we feel the message 'went in one ear and out the other,' and I quote this phrase frequently, 'always seek for understanding, and then seek to be understood.'"

In his years at Minnesota, coach Frost has worked hard to establish a culture of respect. Out of that culture has grown significant trust between Frost and his players. This trust has empowered him to be honest and authentic with his players. Frost says, "I try to keep in mind that 'truth is your best friend.' Real friends will tell you the truth . . . My players know that I have their best interests in mind. Therefore, they can listen to what I say in a better way." Frost's approach to the tough conversations depends on establishing relationships and knowing each player before the tough conversations take place. As a result, his players are more likely to receive his feedback in the spirit it is intended. Coach Spring at Illinois echoes Frost's emphasis on trust and relationships. According to Spring, "If the athlete or person knows your intention is to make them better or help them, they are more likely to open up and have a higher level of disclosure. Then you'll actually be having a conversation."

The desire of every great teacher is for every student to reach his full potential. Teaching certainly would be easier if every student learned the same way, developed at the same rate, and enjoyed the same capacity for achievement. As with athletes, though, students vary greatly in the way they learn and the speed at which they learn, as well as the highest level of achievement each is capable of reaching. Therefore, a great teacher can't always communicate with a broad, one-size-fits-all approach and expect individuals to respond in a way that prompts learning, growth, and development. A great teacher, like a great coach, must work one-on-one with each student as often as possible to provide specific feedback and instruction. Many times these conversations involve positive feedback in the form of congratulations, gold stars, and encouragement. Often, though, these conversations involve addressing mistakes students make, work habits, and other growth areas in which students must make progress to continue achieving at a desirable level. Simply put, these conversations can be just as challenging and no more fun than similar conversations between coach and player on the field or court. Thankfully, there's a proven model for how to set such conversations up to be successful and meaningful in the classroom.

Frost's approach provides a great model for teachers in the classroom. Just as Frost and Spring work to build a relationship with their athletes, so must a great teacher. Most students will be guarded or defensive and not open to feedback from a teacher when the time comes for honest assessment and feedback on growth areas. Just like athletes, most students don't like to hear about their weaknesses or areas that need improvement. However, when a great teacher establishes a positive healthy relationship before the tough conversations take place, a student will be less defensive and will be less likely to perceive the feedback as negative or critical. When a student realizes that, like Frost's players and Spring's athletes, the teacher has his best interests in mind, he can listen to what the teacher says in a better way.

While it may seem obvious, it is worth pointing out that there are two sure-fire ways a student can know that a teacher has his best interests in mind, not only during tough conversations but in the classroom daily. First, a great teacher states this clearly and states this often. A student should know a teacher has his best interests in mind because he hears her tell him so in no uncertain terms. A student needs to hear this from his teacher because he may not hear it anywhere else. Second, a great teacher demonstrates through her actions that her students' best interests are always front and center, and that her students' best interests drive everything she does in the classroom. Students of all ages are intuitive and they will know if this is, in fact, what motivates their teacher. Saying so is easy, but proving to students daily that she is looking out for their best interests can create a powerful bond between the teacher and her students, regardless of their ages. These two pieces of the puzzle are the keys to building relationships based on trust and respect both in the athletic arena and in the classroom. Whether students realize it or not, part of looking out for their best interests involves a willingness to have one-on-one, often tough, conversations with students. Without intentionality heading into these conversations, as both Frost and Spring will attest, tough conversations either won't go well or won't happen at all in either the classroom or the sports world. Tough, one-on-one conversations from honest, trusted coaches and teachers must occur; otherwise, neither athletes nor students will ever reach their full potential.

8

Do Something Different

> **"** If you want something different, *do* something different. Without change, progress is impossible. **"**
>
> (Steve Maraboli)

Sometimes everything works. Sometimes kids hang on every word, follow instructions perfectly, focus completely on the task at hand, and master new concepts quickly and easily. Sometimes kids execute mistake-free drills, produce personal bests, and exceed expectations. And, on the other hand, sometimes nothing works. Sometimes kids zone out, stare blankly as if instructions were being given in a different language, lose focus almost instantly, and struggle with anything new. Sometimes kids make mistake after mistake, fail miserably, and miss the mark entirely. Any coach or teacher looks brilliant when everything works, but what's to be done when nothing works?

When coaches and teachers find themselves in situations where nothing seems to work, a number of easy options often seem rather tempting. For example, a coach introduces to a basketball team a new fast-break drill designed to lay the groundwork for a new fast-break offense, but the players seem dumbfounded, confused, or overwhelmed. As the players' frustration grows, more than likely so does the coach's frustration, and the coach may be tempted to stay with what he's doing longer than he should. The coach may be tempted to dig in his heels and tell the players that they'll run the drill until they get it right regardless of how many times it takes. The coach may dole out punishment for every time a player or players get it wrong. The coach may end practice abruptly and tell the players they'd better have it figured out when they return to practice the next day. The coach may even throw a fit and decide to drop the idea altogether.

Similar options might tempt teachers when they find themselves in just such a situation. If a teacher introduces a new concept, like multiplying and dividing numbers with exponents, and students stare back with befuddled looks, a teacher might opt for one of the following approaches. Tempted to stick with what she's doing longer than is healthy, the teacher may want to work more and more problems, or assign more for homework, convinced that the more the students do these problems the more likely they are to figure out the concept. The teacher may take points off every time students get a problem wrong as a way to motivate them. The teacher may shut the book, turn off the projector, and tell the students to figure it out on their own time. The teacher may even want to just say "forget it" and move on to something else. Hopefully that would not happen, but in moments of frustration it may be tempting.

A good coach or teacher knows that none of these options produce the desired results. None of these options lead to mastery of concepts, proficiency with certain skills, or improved performance. The easy thing to do, especially for someone who might be tired or frustrated, is to choose one of these options and shift the responsibility to the learners. There's a better way to handle things when nothing seems to work. Whether on the court or in the classroom, when nothing seems to work, the coach or teacher must call a timeout to sort things out and assess the situation. When faced with such a dilemma, a good coach or teacher first senses the frustration of the learners. Their frustration serves as the indicator that something isn't working, that there's a disconnect and learning isn't happening. The next step for either a good coach or teacher will not be to pound the concept into the learners or get upset and quit, but rather to try to pinpoint the disconnect between teacher and learners. When players aren't mastering skills and performing up to potential, a good coach looks first at himself. Likewise, when a student struggles, a good teacher looks at herself first.

An oft-quoted proverb, usually and mistakenly attributed to Albert Einstein, says, "Insanity is doing the same thing over and over again but expecting different results." The key to fixing the "nothing's working" situation, therefore, lies first in asking the question, "Am I really trying many approaches and in fact nothing's working, or am I doing and saying the same thing over and over and expecting learning to happen?" A good coach or teacher knows that when nothing seems to work, it just feels that way to both teacher and learner. Something will work. In reality, nothing has worked *yet*. The coach or teacher first needs to try a different approach. If a new approach also fails to produce the desired results, it may be time to call in backup.

Only a confident coach or teacher can ask the tough question, realize his or her approach isn't working, and step aside to make way for someone or something else. For the frustrated coach, the solution to "nothing's working" may be as simple as bringing in another coach to explain the same drill in different terms. The solution may be as simple as having a player explain the drill differently to the other players. Maybe a video clip or software animation of the desired outcome will do the trick. For the frustrated teacher, perhaps asking a colleague how he or she might explain the concept will bring a fresh perspective and a solution to the problem. The solution in the classroom, as on the basketball court, may be as simple as having a student teach the concept to the rest of the class. An instructional video, perhaps from Kahn Academy or a similar site, may make the light bulb turn on for everyone, students and teacher alike.

Even the best coaches and teachers occasionally feel like nothing's working. When good coaches and teachers encounter this frustrating feeling, they remember what Einstein apparently didn't say and they do something different. They may change their own approach, ask others to weigh in, or use an outside source to illustrate what they're teaching. Good coaches and teachers know that not changing something when nothing's working certainly will lead to insanity.

9

A Sign of Things to Come

> **"**The philosophy behind much advertising
> is based on the old observation that
> every man is really two men –
> the man he is and the man he wants to be.**"**
>
> (William Feather)

Many great coaches have learned a valuable marketing lesson and have applied that lesson to their teams and organizations. What lesson is that? A powerful motivational sign – emblazoned with a motto, mission, or vision – can help shape and define the culture of a team or organization. Locker-room speeches, no matter how powerful, come and go. Pre-game and halftime speeches also come and go. A smart motivational sign, however, posted in a strategic location for all to see serves as a powerful reminder for all who pass. In terms of external communication, a great sign serves as a very public statement about what is important to that team or organization. In terms of internal communication, such a sign can remind the organization's members of its mission statement, motto, slogan, rallying cry, core values, and more. When such a sign falls in line with what the organization holds dear, even the sign itself, and not just its message, can become engrained in the organization's culture and can help define or redefine the culture for all future members.

If the hype about the power of a sign sounds too easy or too cliché, consider one of the greatest and most famous motivational signs hanging on any wall anywhere in the sports world: "Play like a champion today." Notre Dame football players pass beneath that sign every time they take the field. For the Notre Dame faithful, it is more than just a sign, though. It is a belief statement, a mission statement, a statement of core values, and a set of goals all rolled into one. The sign echoes what the Notre Dame coaching staff preach daily. The sign echoes what Notre Dame alum have come to expect of current and future players. The sign mirrors the culture of the organization. The sign reminds players that along with the privilege of wearing the gold helmet comes the responsibility to strive to play at a certain level, at a very high level, at a championship level. If you think this is just a sign, a sign with little to no meaning, think again. People across the globe know this sign, though few actually have laid eyes on it.

Notre Dame does not hold a monopoly on motivational signs that communicate values to those both within and outside a particular organization. Plenty of other coaches and teams use similar signs, signs tied directly to a team motto, a core value, or the like. Consider these signs heralding the value of hard work: "Be proud of the way we work," used by the Pittsburgh Penguins hockey team; "When you're not practicing, someone else is," at Georgia Tech; "Train Hard," at Purdue University; and "Prep not Hype," from Lane Kiffin's days at USC. Similarly, these powerful signs give the clarion call to dedication and commitment: "Those who stay will be champions," at the University of Michigan; "What you gave today, you have; what you didn't give, you've lost forever," from the University of Missouri; and "Finish the Drill," from the University of Georgia. Some great motivational signs take a slightly more cerebral approach: "Victory favors the team that makes the fewest mistakes," from the University of Iowa; and "The arrogance of success is to think that what you did yesterday will be good enough for tomorrow," used by the Buffalo Bills football team. Each of these signs provides a rallying point for players, coaches, the team, and, in fact, the entire organization. These signs hold value because they have become part of the culture of the organizations.

The items hanging on the walls of schools and classrooms say as much about those schools' communities and classrooms as locker-room signs say about the teams and organizations above. Visitors to a school or classroom will walk away with an impression of what the school or teacher stands for, believes in, and values. Faculty and students who walk the halls and visit classrooms also will have an impression of what the school or teacher holds dear. Why leave anything to chance or interpretation? As one descends the stairs to head toward the Notre Dame football field, there can be no question about what the program values and expects. The same should be true for every school and every classroom. Plenty of schools and classrooms already post vision statements, honor codes, mission statements, motivational thoughts, and more. Plenty do not.

A great teacher should seize the opportunity to proudly display for her students what she believes and values. Posting the school mission statement or vision is a great place to start. Likewise, posting the school's honor code, if the school has one, is a great way to show support for the school and the things it values. A great teacher should go a step further, though. A teacher passionate about creativity should reflect that on her walls. A teacher who incessantly preaches hard work should say so in more ways than just through the spoken word. A teacher wanting to promote kindness or respect should have that represented somewhere in the room for all the students and classroom visitors to see. Hanging posters or signs in a classroom may seem like a small, insignificant gesture, but this simple action virtually guarantees students will be reminded of the message 180 times. These messages help students and visitors get to know the teacher and communicate the expectations or values they can expect to experience while in the classroom. Talk about bang for the buck! Even when students seem to tune the teacher out, they often scour classroom walls and absorb whatever is there. Get the message to the captive audience! Just as the motto "Work Hard. Be Nice." has become central to the culture of KIPP schools across America – because the schools proudly display the words everywhere and refer to them daily – the same phenomenon can happen in any school or classroom. When a great teacher's values, expectations, or vision hang prominently in her classroom, her students can't help but notice and be at least a little affected. As an added bonus, her students just might be challenged and inspired, too.

Section II

Harness the Power of Teamwork

1

Giving Ownership to the Team

> **"** I have tried a number of methods to build
> teamwork, but I believe the thing that worked
> best for me was stressing the tradition of our
> program and the responsibility that each team
> has to continue that tradition. If we worked
> together, we could continue to build
> on that tradition, but if we chose to be
> individuals we would fail to meet our goals. **"**
>
> (*Dale Monsey*, retired Texas high school
> basketball coach, 500+ wins)

When Duke University men's basketball coach Mike Krzyzewski took the reins of the US men's national basketball team in 2005, he faced an interesting challenge. Ever since changes were made that allowed NBA players to play on the US men's national basketball team, USA Basketball teams played less like unified teams and more like collections of individual players focused on individual goals. NBA players had a reputation for being free-spirited, egotistical, and not particularly interested in teamwork, and Krzyzewski had been charged with molding these egos into a unit that would win as a team. These egos included NBA personalities Carmelo Anthony, Kobe Bryant, Dwight

Howard, LeBron James, Chris Paul, Dwyane Wade, and more. How would Krzyzewski, also known as "Coach K," wrangle these individuals and transform them into a team?

Coach K could have walked into the first practice with his new players and laid down the law. He easily could have presented his players with lists of rules and threatened his players with consequences if they didn't get on the same page quickly and compliantly. Wisely, Coach K knew better than to approach this group of individuals in such a way. Coach K, instead, called a team meeting. In his quiet, calm way, he presented to his players the pressures and challenges that lay ahead of them. He then asked the players to do something simple but remarkable. Coach K asked this group of extremely talented individuals to set team goals and to present to him the policies and procedures the team would need in order to accomplish those goals. His new players responded exactly as he'd hoped.

Predictably, the players wanted nothing less than a gold-medal run through the Olympic Games. Then, one by one, these stars raised their hands and offered suggestions as to how they would reach that goal. "We'll have no bad practices," one offered. "No one will be late to practice," offered another. And so it went. The players themselves created the same policies and procedures Coach K would have created for the team. What made these different than if Coach K had walked in and written them on the board for the team? Coach K gave the players ownership of the entire process. Rather than goading them into becoming invested, he allowed and empowered the players to decide to become invested.

Mick Haley, the women's volleyball coach at the University of Southern California, knows more than a little about teamwork, too. With six junior college national championships, four NCAA national championships, and well over 1,000 career wins, Haley understands the value of teamwork. He also knows how to teach it and how to harness the power of teamwork. "In my sport, teamwork is essential," says Haley. "Therefore, everyone needs to be involved in setting the culture, rules, and all things pertinent to success. Each player then has to commit to buying in. Respect, trust, effort, attitude, enthusiasm are all part of the buy-in. Having a team develop this is where you get the best opportunity for teamwork."

Haley's and Coach K's wisdom easily translates to the classroom. Education books, blogs, and conferences have been buzzing in recent years about the power of giving students choice and ownership in the learning process. Students of all ages, literally from kindergarten to twelfth grade, respond favorably to policies, procedures, rules, assignments, assessments, and projects when provided the opportunity to make choices about them. Similarly, students buy in, to borrow words from Haley, to the classroom culture when they have some ownership in establishing the culture.

School children of all ages often follow classroom rules and procedures more consistently when they're given the opportunity to collaboratively contribute to the rules and procedures. Often, students' expectations of themselves and one another exceed those of the adults around them when those students are given ownership. This comes as no surprise to Haley, as this is the approach he uses with his elite athletes, too. His advice is, "You have to identify all the things that you want in your culture, and I would recommend the players or learners have some input into this process. We evaluate this yearly and tweak it accordingly to the learners' needs. Once the culture is established, the work ethic is not a problem." Elementary students' eyes light up when given the chance to choose which learning centers to explore, which animal to read about, or which book to pull from the shelves. Middle and high school students, especially, become more engaged in learning when allowed to select from an assortment of projects or assessments, choose their own literature for reading, or select a topic of interest to them for research or for experimentation.

When teachers allow students to have a voice, students take ownership. When students take ownership, they become invested and take pride in the process and the outcomes, just as Haley's players have and Coach K's players did in the Olympics. At the end of the day, Coach K still reserved the right to make decisions and call the shots that affected the wellbeing of the team, just as a teacher does in the classroom. However, Haley and Coach K each empowered his players to have a more meaningful and successful experience by giving them a voice, thus allowing them to take ownership.

NBA and Olympic basketball star Kobe Bryant said of the process with Coach K, "We all jelled together as a team." Even though the collection of NBA stars, so often beguiled for their egos, played fewer minutes than most members of the other Olympic teams, the motley crew came together under Coach K's leadership to win all eight Olympic basketball games in 2008, including the gold-medal game against Spain. Haley's teams have amassed more than 1,000 wins and ten national titles. Imagine the new heights students could reach under the leadership of teachers who allowed students to make choices in the learning process.

2

Getting Results by Assigning Roles

> 66 People who work together will win,
> whether it be against complex football
> defenses, or the problems of modern society. 99

(Vince Lombardi, legendary NFL coach,
six-time NFL champion, and two-time
Super Bowl champion)

If a number of kids gather to play an impromptu pickup game on a beach, in a sandlot, on a playground, or in a park, more players than not will scramble to be pitcher, quarterback, outside hitter, center forward, goalie, or point guard. Conversely, few if any of the players likely will want dibs on right field, left tackle, small forward, or right back. Naturally, every kid in the group will gravitate toward the most glamorous, highest-profile positions on the court or field regardless of what skills he has to offer the team. Furthermore, the kids then will sort themselves into loosely organized, lopsided teams, and it's a safe bet that the skills and talents of the players on each team will not be utilized effectively. Once the fun begins, the actual gameplay probably will be dominated by one or two players on each team who will get all or almost all the touches on the ball. This should come as no surprise. Left on their own to assign roles in a group, kids often exhibit this predictable behavior. While such teams might be acceptable for a Sunday afternoon of recreational fun, they won't be efficient or balanced, they won't highlight each player's strengths, and they certainly won't win any league championships.

Admittedly, teams organized in such a way aren't competing for championships, but this scenario illustrates the natural tendency of kids of all ages when left to organize themselves into groups. As Pepperdine men's volleyball coach *Marv Dunphy* says, players need to experience "diffused friendship patterns" as members of a team and they need to not be allowed to fall into their normal cliques. This scenario also demonstrates one of the most important responsibilities of a good coach.

Young athletes, and arguably athletes of all ages, wanting to perform their best as a team need an objective third party to organize them. They need a good coach to help sort out players' skills, talents, strengths, and weaknesses, and then assign roles accordingly. Says Dunphy, "Part of being a good coach, a good leader, a good parent is having the courage to make the tough decision, to provide role clarity, and to give them [players] what you perceive their role to be." A good coach understands the importance of assessing players' strengths, and then assigning roles on the team that accentuate the players' strengths. Likewise, a good coach understands the importance of identifying players' weaknesses and considering those weaknesses when assigning roles on the team so the players' weaknesses can be minimized or compensated for. Just as a team benefits when players enjoy opportunities to play to their strengths, a team suffers when players must struggle with their weaknesses more often than is necessary. The coach then can help each player know his or her role. Only when a player knows his role can he be most productive. If a player doesn't know his role, how will he know what he's expected to contribute to the team effort?

In terms of productivity, balance may be just as important to a team's success as the talent level of individual players. In other words, a team works best when various talents and skills are distributed evenly and appropriately across the court or field. A good coach understands this and organizes his teams, lineups, and practice squads according to this principle. A great offensive line is worth its weight in gold (and that's a lot of gold) in the football world, but even 11 exceptional offensive linemen on the field at the same time against a balanced football team will struggle to score a single point or keep opponents from scoring at will. In basketball, the point guard position requires great skill, but the five best point guards in the country probably could not come together as a winning basketball team. How will the point guards defend against towering centers or snatch rebounds from the power forwards of opposing teams? The six best setters in the nation, when combined on the same volleyball team, stand no chance against decent opponents. A team of great setters may set the ball expertly, but who on the team will deliver crushing attacks? Eleven center forwards may provide a powerful offensive unit as a soccer team, but who will play defense and tend the goal with equal skill? A good coach weighs players' strengths as well as a team's needs, then formulates a lineup that highlights players' strengths and minimizes players' shortcomings while maintaining overall balance and equilibrium. A team assembled with player skill and team balance in mind stands a better chance of success and high productivity than a team centered on individuals' talent alone.

With collaborative learning becoming more widely accepted as good classroom pedagogy, teachers should consider the goal of each collaborative session before groups and teams are assigned. Teachers can organize students any number of ways, but organization should be done with the end product in mind. Group structure may not be much of an issue if students are doing labs, working problems, doing research, or some other activity in the classroom. In these examples, allowing students to self-select groups may be fine. Giving students opportunities to self-select groups and self-assign roles within groups can be a nice change of pace, as well as a good way to give students choice and ownership in their learning. Younger and middle-grade students, however, nearly always divide into groups based on which of their friends can be in the group. These groups aren't always the best for learning or for productivity. Long-term projects that require extended collaboration or work outside of class could be problematic if the groups are not carefully managed.

When productivity becomes a high priority in the process of collaborative learning, students need help with getting organized and selecting roles. A good teacher approaches collaborative learning much the same way as a good coach organizes his team and his line-ups. A good teacher hoping to maximize productivity and efficiency should create groups and assign roles to group members.

Young students in particular need a good teacher to assess the strengths of each student and create balanced groups. A good teacher will not put all the creative, "right-brained" students in one group and put all the black-and-white, "left-brained" students in another group. A good teacher will not create groups of introverts only or extroverts only. Students need a good teacher who knows them well, who can identify strengths and weaknesses, and who can sort them into equi-table, balanced groups. Additionally, students need a good teacher to assign roles within the group based on strengths or skills.

Like a good coach selecting players for a starting lineup, a good teacher assembles groups with balance in mind. A good basketball coach will not send his five best rebounders into the game at the same time because in order to be successful the team needs a passer and ballhandler, a shooter or two, and so on. The same principle applies to teachers organizing students into groups for collaborative learning. A teacher assigns a group project to the class, for example, and challenges each group of four students to create an original movie. The project rubric requires the group to write and storyboard the plot, design cos-tumes, act out the scenes, record the action, and edit the video. First, a good teacher ensures that each group is equitable and balanced. Next, a good teacher works with each group and helps each student under-stand the group's goal as well as how each group member will help contribute so the group can reach the goal. This may require the teacher to assign roles so the group can be most efficient and most productive. Not every student can write the script and not every student can edit the video. Even though every member may contribute to each of the tasks, the best writer probably should oversee the script, the most tech-savvy student should edit the video, and so on. Each student needs to know his or her role. (True, there may be projects where one of the desired outcomes is for each student to get out of his comfort zone and try something new and risky, but the focus right now is on productivity.)

When players and students know their roles within a group, they can focus on what they do best. Point guards don't need to worry much about crashing the boards and battling the big men for rebounds. Instead, under the direction of a good coach, point guards know their energy needs to be devoted to dribbling and advancing the ball up the court and making good passes to open players who can score. In a group project like the one mentioned above, the video editor doesn't need to spend time proofreading the script and the storyboarder doesn't need to worry about costume design. Under the tutelage of a good teacher, the costume designer can be free to focus on costume design and the script writer can spend his time developing the script.

Accountability for individuals within a group can be a challenge unless roles have been assigned and group members know their roles. When coaches and teachers assign roles, accountability becomes much more manageable. If a quarterback has been sacked six times in the first half, the coach probably needs to talk to the offensive line and not the linebackers. If a baseball team has allowed baserunners to steal second base five times in the first five innings, the coach needs to talk to his pitcher, his catcher, and some of his infielders, not his outfielders. With the movie project, the teacher and the other group members know who to turn to if the costumes lack imagination or the script is filled with poor grammar.

When it comes to team or group effort, maximum productivity and efficiency occur when good coaches and teachers organize young people into groups based on strengths, assign roles so the group is balanced, and help students understand their roles. When left on their own to self-select groups and self-assign roles, players and students alike rarely will do so in a way that a good coach or teacher would. Therefore, players and students need good coaches and teachers to be an honest, objective third party capable of assessing each player or student and putting each in a position to be most successful as a team member. When each team member is in the best position to be successful, or in a position to use his or her strengths and talents, the team then will have its best chance at productivity and success.

3

Capitalizing on Shared Values

66 We came up with some values or pillars for our
program: being tough, grateful, disciplined and
devoted. These are not just words on the wall.
These are things our players and staff exude
on a daily basis. We will measure our
success according to our values. When we try
to live out our values every day, **99**
that is when we have a truly great experience.

> (*Brad Frost*, head coach of the two-time
> NCAA national champion University
> of Minnesota women's ice hockey team)

Ask anyone who coaches a team sport, at any level, about the greatest challenge year in and year out, and you probably will hear an answer related to teamwork. Herding a half-dozen four-year-olds on the soccer field into anything that resembles a team or a unit, well . . . good luck. Finding a way to coax five second-grade girls into playing like a legitimate basketball team requires plenty of clear and simple teaching, repetition of drills, and abundant patience. Getting eight-year-old boys to play baseball as a team takes tremendous work, simple instructions, and patience. Training teenagers of either gender to successfully communicate and play like a team on the basketball court demands great instruction and countless hours of practice. Bringing together great individual players from high school to form a successful collegiate team requires everything already mentioned – quality teaching, tremendous work, countless hours of practice, and plenty of patience. In the world of team sports, the best and most productive teams function as a unit, and the teamwork that makes unity possible must be strategically and intentionally emphasized over and over again.

Of all the team sports, perhaps no sport requires teamwork for success more than volleyball. Just ask Bret Almazan-Cezar, the head volleyball coach at Archbishop Mitty High School in San Jose, California, and former American Volleyball Coaches Association Coach of the Year. During his tenure at Mitty, Almazan-Cezar has led his teams to an astounding seven CIF state championships and a top national ranking in 2012. For Almazan-Cezar, teamwork centers on values that every player on the team embraces. He says, "To teach teamwork, one must create a situation where the team has shared values for which to strive, like a pledge of allegiance or a constitution. At Mitty, we have a program prayer that is recited on game days that states our values. It was written by our athletes and has been amended by our athletes. Furthermore, we have a commitment that is recited every day:

> As I step onto this line, I commit myself to this team.
>
> I pledge to act selflessly with integrity and unfailing spirit.
>
> I promise that I will do my best and never give up.
>
> I will strive to compete and reach for the stars."

Heather Tarr, softball coach at the University of Washington, concurs with Almazan-Cezar. Tarr, who has led her Huskies to 20 consecutive NCAA Tournament appearances, 11 Women's College World Series appearances, and an NCAA national championship, says, "Winning traditions come from winning belief systems. As a coach, you must work together with your team and staff to come up with a system that is shared and concrete. Your team members should be able to speak easily to outsiders on what the core beliefs and core covenants are." Tarr echoes Almazan-Cezar regarding the intentionality of teaching values and incorporating them into the daily routine. "We use many creative ways to establish our core beliefs," says Tarr, "but the best teams we have had at Washington [resulted from] the seniors and coaches working together to teach our core values and beliefs to the new players."

For Almazan-Cezar, Tarr, and other great coaches, values like commitment, integrity, effort, and competitiveness must be central to the team or organization. Even with such team values front and center, though, teamwork doesn't happen automatically. Great coaches like Almazan-Cezar and Tarr must incorporate the values daily into their teaching. "We teach our values, and our expectations are pointed at making our values reality. When that happens, everything else comes into place, including the winning," says Almazan-Cezar. "But the focus is never on winning. It's about living the values." In addition to teaching the values, great coaches must give players a chance to demonstrate the values individually and, most importantly, as members of a team. If not for these practice opportunities created strategically and intentionally by great coaches, how else will teamwork become a reality? Almazan-Cezar provides opportunities every day for his players to demonstrate the team values and develop teamwork skills by placing them in both competitive and cooperative situations. "I firmly believe that's what sport is all about," says Almazan-Cezar.

The Partnership for 21st Century Skills lists collaboration as one of the skills that will "separate students who are prepared for increasingly complex life and work environments in today's world and those who are not." Whereas a coach may refer to individuals working together as teamwork, a teacher may describe the process as collaboration. Fostering collaboration, or teamwork, in the classroom can prove just as challenging as on the athletic field. Fortunately for classroom teachers, the model used by Almazan-Cezar works as well in the classroom as it does on the volleyball court, regardless of the age of the students.

A great teacher can follow Almazan-Cezar's model during collaborative work with a little planning and forethought. Once groups or teams have been formed within the classroom, the teacher should emphasize the value or values that will be central to the collaborative experience. The younger the students are, the fewer values should be emphasized; older students can focus on more values per project or assignment. Using the Mitty volleyball team's recited commitment, for example, a teacher can emphasize commitment to the team, or commitment to the group. In this case, the focus can be on every team member working diligently to make the collaborative project successful. Focusing on this value opens the door for a great teacher to discuss work ethic, getting along with one another, everyone pitching in, and more. Drawing again on Mitty's commitment, a teacher could emphasize integrity as the value for a collaborative effort and use that value as a jumping-off point for conversations about academic integrity, doing one's own work, fair use of outside resources, digital citizenship, and more. Finally, if a teacher chooses for a really challenging or difficult project to emphasize the values of doing one's best and never giving up, she has opened the door to tackle life lessons like grit, resilience, and rising to a challenge. In each of these examples, if the students involved in the collaborative work commit to the value, the experience will be more meaningful and more successful.

Almazan-Cezar's emphasis on "living the values" instead of winning merits consideration for classroom work, too. The parallel between the volleyball court and the classroom in this example makes a great deal of sense. If a teacher can focus each group on a few values and have the team members commit to those values, success will be a by-product of a meaningful growth experience in the same way winning has been a by-product of Tarr's and Almazan-Cezar's teaching. That the players themselves have helped build the framework for the team's values makes the process all the more significant and impactful. How powerful would it be to have collaborative work in classrooms guided not only by shared value, but guided by shared values chosen by the students? Under the direction of a great teacher, incredibly so.

The Team Approach to
Time Management

" Is what I'm doing or about to do **"**
getting us closer to our objective?

(Robert Townsend)

Good time management may well be one of the most important skills students can learn in the twenty-first century. Disorganized consumers can find scores of books on time management in bookstores and even more apps to help with time management in app stores. Time management takes practice, though, and the sooner people learn time-management skills, the better off they will be. If students can learn basic time-management principles beginning at an early age, all the better. Most approaches to teaching and emphasizing time management focus on the cost to the individual for poor time management. Taking a page from Mike Krzyzewski's playbook once again, coaches and teachers can find a different approach to teaching time management.

Coach K, Duke men's basketball coach, emphasizes the importance of time management to his players regularly. When he teaches time management, though, he focuses on each player's responsibility to the team. He doesn't emphasize the personal cost of poor time management, but rather the cost to the team if a team member gets himself in a bind because of poor time management. Coach K understands the power of positive peer pressure and he uses that to his advantage. By couching time management as a skill that can help or hurt a player's teammates, he presents time management in such a way that his players do not want to let one another down. For a collegiate basketball player, time management can affect academics, weightroom workouts, team practices, individual skill workouts, and more. Using academics as an example, a player who falls behind in his studies, misses class, allows his grades to drop, or makes poor academic choices that have serious consequences may become ineligible. An ineligible player certainly lets down the team by putting his teammates in a position to have to carry his share of the load in practices and in games.

A savvy classroom teacher can draw on Coach K's wisdom and use the team approach for teaching time management in her classroom. Regardless of their ages, school-age children can work collaboratively, though the potential complexity of the collaboration can increase as the students get older. Whether second graders or sophomores, students involved in collaborative learning should function much like a team. A savvy teacher approaching collaborative work as teamwork can capitalize on the power of positive peer pressure, then, and emphasize the importance of good time management. Good time management helps the group deliver quality work on time and the team experiences success. Poor time management, on the other hand, leads to missed deadlines, rushed or sloppy work, inequitable distribution of responsibilities, and ultimately some amount of failure for the team. Because teams want to be successful and team members want to experience success, team members can put positive pressure on one another and hold one another accountable in ways that a teacher may not.

In terms of equipping students to manage time well, a good teacher can provide individual students and teams with a number of options to help them manage their time. A timeline or calendar that is clearly marked with checkpoints and deadlines can be valuable for students of all ages. A set of written goals and expectations for both the team and team members can provide a tool to help team members keep one another on task and on track. If the collaborative task involves deliverables, a timeline for delivery of the items can be invaluable. By providing these and other tools, a teacher can get students on track at a very early age for good time-management skills. By couching time management in terms of how the students' teammates or peers may be affected, a savvy teacher can leverage students' desires to not let down their peers and build a foundation for good time-management skills that students will need long after they have moved on from school.

Section III

Make Work Meaningful

1

Touches on the Ball

> **“**Probably the single most important thing
> a child can learn in soccer is to be
> comfortable with the ball at their feet.
> And the most effective way to establish
> and enhance that comfort is to give
> them multiple touches on the ball . . .**”**

(from www.backof thenet.com,
authorunknown)

In the world of coaching soccer, player skill development comes down to touches on the ball. The terms of art "touches on the ball" and "ball touches" refer specifically to how many times a player actually touches a soccer ball either during practice time or during a game. As the science of coaching soccer has grown and evolved over the last few generations, the most effective soccer coaches in the world have learned that there is a direct correlation between touches on the ball and player growth. The more meaningful touches on the ball a soccer player has, the more adept the player will become at dribbling, shooting, passing, juggling, and more. The National Soccer Coaches Association of

America (NSCAA) states on its website under "Coaching Points to Consider":

◆ "Use activities that give the player many touches on the ball."
◆ "Develop drills in which each player has a ball and avoid standing in lines."

An effective soccer coach, at any level, embraces these two points and makes them central to every practice. Keeping in mind that players develop their skills according to how many ball touches they get – both during practice and on their own – an effective coach designs an efficient practice during which players have a plethora of meaningful touches on the ball. To do so, an effective coach includes both individual and group drills that put players in contact with the ball often. The more players stand in line, the fewer touches each player gets. The more time the team stands around and watches one or two others do a drill or practice a skill, the fewer touches each player gets.

An effective soccer coach develops ways to keep practice moving at a brisk pace with varied, meaningful activities involving a ball. The skill of dribbling provides a great example. In soccer, dribbling involves a player advancing the ball around the field with his feet, specifically using multiple small and controlled kicks (touches on the ball). Dribbling the ball at a jog across an empty field doesn't require much skill. However, dribbling a ball at a dead run, on a field with 11 fast and aggressive opposing players determined to take the ball away, requires great skill. During practice, a soccer coach could very easily line up the entire team on one end of the soccer field, with each player using his own ball, and have them dribble up and down the field indefinitely. This activity may help some players with the most basic dribbling skills, but it doesn't challenge every player and it doesn't prepare them for a real-game situation. A coach could add a line of cones and require the players to swerve in and out of the cones like a slalom, but this improves the drill only slightly. An effective coach creates a series of drills that progresses from the two just mentioned to a scenario that involves lots of players, each with his own ball, in a limited space with players trying to steal soccer balls. If a coach does this, he's created both variety and meaningfulness in his drills, and he's provided his players maximum touches on the ball.

The NSCAA adds two other significant teaching points, among others, to the "Coaching Points to Consider," both of which also affect players' touches on the ball:

- "Coaches should avoid too much talking or lecturing."
- "Practices should be dynamic and full of action to maximize limited time and keep the interest of the players."

For every minute a coach talks and lectures, a minute passes during which players get no touches on the ball. Granted, there are times when coaches need to provide direct instruction, but the NSCAA doesn't warn against that. Rather, the NSCAA discourages "too much talking or lecturing." Furthermore, practices that aren't "dynamic and full of action" will be slow-moving affairs that do not resemble real-game situations. Chances are that players will have fewer touches on the ball in static, slow-moving practices during which a coach drones on and on. Since more touches on the ball result in greater player development, an effective coach avoids such practices at all costs.

An effective teacher understands the premise of touches on the ball for developing her students. Students need hands-on practice and activities in order to develop their skills and proficiencies, and an effective teacher will work hard to provide those opportunities. Just hands-on activities will not do, though. Students need varied and meaningful activities that provide the equivalent of touches on the ball that prepare them for real-game situations.

Consider the example of an elementary teacher teaching students to use a number line. Using a very traditional approach, she could stand at the board and provide direct instruction on how to use a number line. This would be acceptable and even effective for a little while, but certainly not for long. After brief direct instruction, an effective teacher would use a variety of meaningful activities – keeping the class both "dynamic and full of action," as the NSCAA recommends for its coaches – to provide students the touches on the ball, or the hands-on time, they need to prepare them for real-life situations.

Simply handing out worksheets full of number lines won't do. That may be a good start but, like dribbling in a straight line on an open field with no defenders, the exercise neither challenges the students nor gives them training for real-life situations. Having students one at a time go to the board to do number line problems doesn't cut it, either; it's the equivalent of players standing in line waiting for a turn with the ball. An effective teacher creates multiple opportunities for all her students to have varied, meaningful hands-on practice. An effective teacher would have students tackle multiple real-life number line problems ranging from reading temperatures on a thermometer to measuring distances with a yardstick to calculating yards gained and lost on a football field. These activities could be done individually or in groups, but the students would have plenty of hands-on.

The analogy applies equally well to a teacher introducing Shakespeare to her students. Using a traditional approach, the teacher could lecture on the life and times of William Shakespeare, teach the literary elements of one of Shakespeare's plays, and then assign a passage of *Macbeth*, *Hamlet*, or *Romeo and Juliet* for the students to read. While this approach might be acceptable, it falls short. An effective teacher would give her students touches on the ball, or hands-on opportunities with the works of William Shakespeare. Just as an effective coach knows that soccer players need to work with a ball if they're going to improve their soccer skills, an effective teacher knows that students studying Shakespeare must speak and hear the great playwright's masterful language in order to really grasp it. Under the direction of an effective teacher, students could take turns reading aloud, they could act out parts, or they even could memorize soliloquies. The important part of teaching Shakespeare lies not with what the teacher can tell the students but rather with what the students will learn from being actively engaged and involved with a text, or the equivalent of getting touches on the Shakespearean ball.

The recommendations from the NSCAA apply to other classes equally as well as they apply to soccer, elementary math, and even Shakespeare. Writing, vocabulary, second languages, science, map skills, coding, stage acting, and many more topics lend themselves perfectly to the analogy of touches on the ball. An effective teacher, regardless of the subject or age she teaches, makes a habit of keeping classes dynamic and full of action, avoiding too much talking and lecturing, finding ways to provide hands-on learning opportunities, and avoiding situations where her students stand in line to learn, even if she never has stumbled upon the NSCAA website. Central to learning in an effective teacher's classroom, though, remains the concept of touches on the ball.

2

Teaching the "Why?"

> **❝** We speak to 'purpose' with everything we do. In today's world people are just going through the motions with everything they do more than ever . . . It's important to switch things up and frequently bring the 'why' into the daily activities! **❞**
>
> *(Justin Spring*, Olympic bronze medalist and NCAA national champion head coach of men's gymnastics at the University of Illinois)

"Why?" Has any question been asked more often of teachers throughout history? Perhaps "Will this be on the test?" runs a close second, but more than anything else students want to know *why*. Students want to know *why* even more often than they want to know *how*. Why is this true? Humans have been wired to be curious, to look for connections and to find meaning in whatever they do. Students arrive in this world as curious beings and, with the help of parents and effective teachers, that curiosity can endure for a lifetime. Therefore, teachers and coaches alike must be prepared to answer every *why* question asked of them no matter how many times the question is asked. Perhaps more importantly, though, effective coaches and teachers need to teach the *why* before teaching the *how*. Teaching *why* helps players and students understand purpose and make their work meaningful so they understand the meaning of *how*.

America's pastime, the sport of baseball, provides a few great examples of the importance of teaching *why*. Louisiana high school baseball coaching legend *M.L. Woodruff*, who led his team to 11 state championships and over 600 victories, always demonstrated the concept of teaching *why* before *how* with the example of the sacrifice bunt. In baseball, a batter bunts when he squares up to the pitcher and taps or drops the pitched baseball softly into the infield rather than swinging through the ball in order to drive it out into the field of play. In a game where the object of the batter appears to be hitting the ball as hard and far as possible so he can reach base safely, the bunt can seem counter-intuitive. The sacrifice bunt, which requires the batter to intentionally trade an out for advancing a runner already on base, seems even more counter-intuitive. It makes perfect sense, then, for a player to ask *why* when being taught the art of the sacrifice bunt.

When teaching the sacrifice bunt to his players, Woodruff began with the *why*: "The reason for the sacrifice bunt is to give oneself up for the team in order to move a teammate to the next base. By advancing your teammate to the next base, it is easier for him to score a run. Great bunters are usually great team players." Only once his players understood *why* he taught the sacrifice bunt could Woodruff move on to the specifics of *how* to bunt. "When you bunt," Woodruff taught, "make sure that you move up in the batter's box toward the pitcher. You want to be in front of the plate so when you bunt the ball . . ." And so the lesson on *how* to bunt continued. According to Woodruff, "As a coach, it is important to teach the why then the how. The why says to the player and to the team 'this is important.' Good coaches explain the why before the question is ever asked." Imagine how differently his players would have approached the sacrifice bunt had they not understood exactly *why* the sacrifice bunt mattered. Practicing the *how* of the sacrifice bunt became much more meaningful for his players once they understood the *why*.

Woodruff's emphasis on teaching the *why* makes sense for teachers in the classroom. Consider the example of an elementary teacher teaching her class the traditional, vertical algorithm for adding 305 + 168. She will need to explain *why* students carry the 1 after adding the 5 and the 8. If she doesn't, students will be left wondering *why* while trying to master the *how*. Students who never learn the *why* of carrying the 1 will go through the motions without ever truly comprehending and mastering the concept. By explaining the *why* of carrying the 1, the teacher not only contributes to student mastery but also, as Woodruff explained, emphasizes the importance of the concept. When students realize the importance of carrying the 1, their work becomes more meaningful. Countless other examples from any number of academic disciplines could be listed as examples for teaching *why*, but the premise remains the same.

The effective teacher takes the concept of teaching *why* a step further. Woodruff explains, "Good coaches explain the why before the question is ever asked," and this serves as a great strategy for teachers to practice. The savvy teacher, like a good coach, thinks ahead, predicts when and where students will ask *why*, and then explains the *why* before the students ask the question during the process of learning the *how*. Students who understand *why* inevitably will be better and more successful with the *how*. By explaining the *why* before students ask, the effective teacher equips them with confidence, enhances their understanding, and provides them a road map for where the lesson and the work are taking them. The more students understand not only why they are doing what they are doing but also where they are going, the more meaningful their work becomes for them. And, as an added bonus, the more meaningful the work, the less likely students are to ask, "Will this be on the test?"

3

Activity Does Not Equal Achievement

> **"** We avoid spending too much time on any one drill and we try to communicate ahead of time the 'why,' and how we will be doing a certain drill. We tell them (talk), we show them (video or chalk talk) and then we actually do the drill. **"**
>
> *(Terry Schroeder*, coach of Pepperdine University men's water polo, NCAA national champion, and Olympic medalist as athlete and coach)

One of the greatest achievements in all of sport belongs to legendary men's basketball coach John Wooden. Wooden, also known as the "Wizard of Westwood," coached UCLA to ten NCAA championships between 1964 and 1975, and seven consecutive championships between 1967 and 1973. If any coach ever understood achievement, that man was former English teacher John Wooden. Wooden's players remember him as a brilliant coach and teacher who taught them valuable life lessons and provided countless witticisms, maxims, and words of wisdom. It should come as no surprise that one of Wooden's most quoted maxims is, "Don't mistake activity for achievement."

Wooden's UCLA teams famously ran one offense year in and year out. The high-post offense, as it was called, proved to be a highly effective offense for UCLA because it balanced simplicity with flexibility and creative options. Wooden's teams rehearsed and drilled the high-post offense every day in practice until they ran it to perfection. In order to play for Wooden, players had to understand the offense inside and out and execute it flawlessly. To get his players to that level of proficiency, Wooden pushed his players physically and mentally. More importantly, though, Wooden focused on teaching them proper technique with each and every trip they made up and down the court. Wooden knew that running through endless repetitions of high-post drills would not achieve the success he desired. Endless repetitions certainly equaled activity, but that activity did not necessarily equal achievement. Achievement came only when players ran the drills efficiently and correctly with plenty of assessment and feedback from Wooden throughout.

A good coach, regardless of his sport, employs Wooden's approach. Many young, inexperienced, or ineffective coaches, however, mistake activity for achievement. Some coaches fall into the trap of thinking that practice necessarily makes players better and drills necessarily improve skill mastery. These same coaches often see players working hard and assume they are improving. These coaches have missed Wooden's point that only proper, well-designed practice makes players better and only drills done correctly, with corrective feedback from the coach, improve players' skills.

Coaches who mistake activity for achievement often take this faulty logic to the extreme and mistake *more* activity for *more* achievement. If one hour of practice is good, two hours of practice must be better. If shooting 100 free throws in practice improves free-throw shooting percentage, then shooting 300 free throws in practice must yield even better results. Such coaches have missed the point that extra practice just for the sake of practice will not be beneficial and free throws practiced incorrectly, regardless of how many free throws the player shot, will not result in more free throws made. Simply practicing a skill or running a drill will not increase achievement, and neither will practicing or drilling more.

As much as Wooden's wisdom makes sense for basketball and other sports, his maxim makes even more sense in education. Student activity – classroom activities, learning activities, labs, homework, worksheets, reading assignments, writing assignments, verb conjugations, math problems – does not equal student achievement. A good teacher understands Wooden's philosophy and employs Wooden's approach in the classroom. An effective math teacher, for example, realizes that if a student works through an assignment of 20 multiplication problems, the student hasn't necessarily achieved anything, even if the student answers all the problems correctly. A busy student may be achieving nothing other than staying busy. Furthermore, such an assignment accomplishes nothing if the student works many or all of the problems incorrectly. For achievement to occur in this scenario, the student needs time to practice, then corrective feedback on whatever he doesn't understand, followed by the opportunity to practice what he's just been taught, followed again by more feedback. Just as Wooden would correct his players if they ran drills incorrectly, a good teacher assesses student activity intermittently and keeps them on track. Just as a good coach watches drills to check for players' understanding and proper execution, a good teacher does the same with student work.

Just as a good teacher doesn't mistake activity for achievement, a good teacher doesn't mistake *more* activity with *more* achievement. A good teacher avoids the pitfall of believing that if a 20-problem assignment has value then a 40-problem assignment will really increase student achievement because it has twice the value. A good teacher knows that more work, more activity, does not produce more achievement. More math, more writing, more reading, more studying, more homework, and more learning activity may produce nothing other than a student who is busier. Wooden wouldn't have wanted that result for his players and a good teacher doesn't desire that for students.

No evidence exists that indicates either activity equals achievement or more activity equals more achievement. Therefore, the teacher who boasts about the mountains of work she gives her students probably has much in common with the coach who prides himself on long, punishing, extended practices. Both of these examples, and there are plenty like them on the fields and courts and in the classrooms and lecture halls, likely could learn much from effective coaches like Wooden, whose sage advice, "Don't mistake activity for achievement," rings as true in twenty-first-century basketball arenas and classrooms as it did when UCLA dominated men's basketball for more than a decade.

4

Using Formative and Summative Assessments Effectively

> **"** In both coaching and teaching there are learning outcomes and objectives. Coaches, like teachers, must be clear with the learners about what the intended outcomes are, and test the learners to evaluate if the learners have met the objectives. We have to constantly remember as coaches, it's not important how much the coach knows, rather, it's what the student learns that is most important! **"**
>
> (*Heather Tarr*, NCAA national champion with 21 consecutive NCAA Tournament appearances and 11 Women's Softball College World Series appearances as the University of Washington softball coach)

Coaches who aren't well-versed in classroom terms of art may not be familiar with formative and summative assessments. Good coaches, though, whether they know these vocabulary terms or not, use formative and summative assessments frequently and rely on them heavily for measuring player and team progress. The two forms of assessment vary from one another but they both hold great value for player development. One of the foundations of effective teaching and developing players into what they have the potential to become lies in using the two types of assessment correctly.

Formative assessments, regardless of whether they're used with sports teams or academic classes, monitor learning and provide valuable, frequent feedback on strengths, weaknesses, and progress of learners. These assessments equip learners and instructors to target specific areas or skills for extra practice immediately. Formative assessments tend to be frequent, ongoing, or regularly occurring low-stakes assessments that focus on specific skills or proficiencies. In the sports world, practices and scrimmages (practice games or informal games, either inter-squad or intra-squad, that result in neither an official win nor loss) serve as perhaps the best examples of formative assessments.

Summative assessments, which are cumulative, evaluate learning either at the end of a unit, or at a predetermined point in time. Often high-stakes, summative assessments tend to be less specific and require learners to demonstrate a range of skills and knowledge. The results of summative assessments often are compared to a benchmark and serve to prepare both instructor and learners for future work. The best examples from sports include games and tournaments.

Many coaches provide their teams and players with the most instruction during practice time. They also do most assessment during practice time. *Clint Hormann*, athletic technology coordinator and tight ends coach for the 2012 4A state champion football team from Cedar Park High School in Texas, works with his coaching staff daily on formative assessment. Hormann says of the Cedar Park coaching staff, "[We] preview the upcoming team, practice it, reteach, practice and reteach it again . . . If we see something in practice that is not done correctly, we do not move on to new material, we schedule it again for the next practice." The Cedar Park staff also record each practice from four different angles for the purpose of formative assessment and stores the footage using a service called Hudl. "Not a play or small variance in technique gets by those four cameras. This allows us, as coaches, to review practices with our athletes and reteach anything that was executed . . . not so well on the practice field. Having the ability to review practice and teach from it is by far the most important part of what we do as coaches."

Cedar Park High School's use of practice time and video of practices perfectly illustrates formative assessment. Using both firsthand observations on the practice field along with the video recordings of practices, the football coaching staff frequently assess individual players and the team for specific skills and proficiencies. Because the team doesn't earn wins or losses each day in practice, the stakes remain low. Additionally, when the staff identify areas that need extra effort or attention, they can focus on better or different instruction right away to develop their players.

Like good coaches, good teachers make formative assessments part of their regular classroom routine. In the classroom, formative assessments can be as simple and informal as question and answer sessions, students working at the board, students responding with "clickers" (student response systems), short quizzes or other assignments, or even conversations with students as a teacher moves about the classroom. The importance of formative assessments lies not in how often students are assessed or in what ways, but rather the importance lies in what the teacher does with the data. A good teacher acts quickly based on the data collected through formative assessment.

Like other good coaches, Coach Hormann and his fellow coaches rely heavily on summative assessments, as well. Few things in the sports world are as high stakes as Texas high school football, but Cedar Park's staff use Friday night football games as the ultimate summative assessments. "Finally, we have our test. The score represents immediate feedback and the following day during grading they [the players] receive even more feedback. Much like practice video, game video allows us to review our game from the previous day with our athletes. The coaches grade every play on Saturday morning before the athletes arrive and then we watch the game again with them, using our notes from grading to teach them about their technique on each play and how to improve for the following week."

Cedar Park High School uses Friday night football games the same way good teachers use summative assessments in the classroom. The coaching staff assess the players and the team at the end of each week of practice (much like an academic unit) using a high-stakes football game. Whether the team spent the week preparing for a spread offense or a Wing T offense, the coaches assess the team and grade the team's Friday night performance. What Hormann and his fellow coaches do with the graded assessment, though, sets them apart as good teachers, too. The coaches review the assessment and the grading, then use that to teach and reteach the players. As in the classroom, assessments have little or no value when learners receive only a grade and no feedback from the assessment.

Good teachers use summative assessments much the way Cedar Park's football staff use Friday night football games. Good teachers provide meaningful instruction and practice for their students based largely on data collected from formative assessments in order to prepare them for summative assessments. In the classroom, summative assessments can be unit tests, semester exams, state testing, or other assessments such as presentations, projects, or speeches. Good teachers don't give summative assessments then move on to something else without reviewing the summative assessments. Rather, good teachers review summative assessments with their students and provide meaningful, growth-oriented feedback. For example, a good communications teacher would not grade a student's speech without providing the student with feedback. A good communications teacher would record and grade a speech the way Cedar Park's football staff recorded and graded a football game, taking time to "teach them about technique" and "how to improve."

In the sports world and in the classroom, assessments used incorrectly do not lead to growth or learning. Assessments used incorrectly lead only to busywork, paperwork, inefficiency, meaningless grades, and frustrated players and students. Good coaches and teachers know not only when to use formative and summative assessments but also what to do with the assessment data in order to promote learning.

5

The Game is the Best Teacher

" Soccer can only be learned by playing soccer. **"**

(Dettmar Cramer, former FIFA soccer coach,
sometimes referred to as the "Football Professor")

An old and oft-repeated soccer adage says, "The game is the best teacher." In soccer, or football, depending on your locale, the saying carries a great deal of weight and many soccer coaches approach player development with this philosophy in mind. At first glance, the saying may appear drastic or even irrational, but whoever penned this proverb never intended to discount the coach in the process of players learning the game and improving skills. After all, players and teams will not progress without a coach to teach and challenge and assess. An expert in the field, the coach, must be present to break down the game, find teachable moments, and provide appropriate instruction. Players, especially young ones, need a coach to teach proper form and technique, game strategy, and rules of the game. Likewise, players and teams will not improve if all they do is play practice matches and real matches. The finer points of the game can't necessarily be learned in either practice or real matches. Player development must include very intentional drills to develop particular skills and target specific areas in need of improvement.

The philosophy of "The game is the best teacher" affects soccer coaching, especially during practices, in a number of ways. Coaches in many sports coach hard during both practices and games. Soccer coaches, especially those who live by this philosophy, coach hard during practices but remain relatively hands-off during matches. These same coaches know how important it is to teach during practice and to let players figure things out during matches. Proper teaching during practice should empower players to perform in matches. Very intentionally, soccer coaches design practices such that some practice time is devoted to drills, repetition, and specific teaching points, and some practice time is devoted to scrimmage, or simulated matches. Soccer coaches usually begin practices with the drills and teaching points and end practices with the simulated matches. This approach to practice allows players to focus on developing a particular strategy or improving a particular facet of the game, then go straight into a simulated match in which they can use what they just learned.

At the risk of stating the obvious, the statement "The game is the best teacher" places great significance on the game itself. Stated another way by Aristotle, someone who likely did not play soccer, "For the things we have to learn before we can do them, we learn by doing them." Taken literally, this soccer mantra has profound implications: for all the practicing and teaching a soccer coach can orchestrate, players learn more from the game itself than from instruction. How can that be? Quite simply, the game itself cannot be simulated accurately. Neither drills nor simulated game situations nor simulated matches can replicate the speed, intensity, and unpredictability of an actual match against an opponent. Therefore, the best way for players to learn the game of soccer, and to practice the skills and concepts they've been taught, is to play the game.

In a soccer match, a real-life situation, players must react to what the game throws at them. A soccer match forces players to simultaneously think on their feet, be creative, problem-solve as the game presents tests and obstacles, and draw on their training, coaching, and instruction. This combination of challenges teaches players at a level and in a way that coaches can't. In a soccer match, players must apply all that they've learned and they learn by virtue of experiencing the match. Furthermore, there is no better way to assess a player's development and progress than with a real-life match. If practice doesn't accurately replicate a match, then real assessment can't take place in practice. Real assessment, taking accurate stock of a player's strengths and weaknesses, must happen in a real-life match.

If "the game" can be translated as "a real-life situation," then the old soccer adage applies equally well to learning and teaching in the classroom as well as outside the classroom. Just as with the soccer coach, the statement "The game is the best teacher" does not discount the value of the classroom teacher or her importance to the development of a student. No one can discount the importance of a teacher to a student learning to read, learning to do long division, learning to compose a paragraph, or learning the unit circle. A student needs an expert to provide both instruction and feedback in each of the aforementioned examples for the proper growth and development to occur. As with coaching, though, there exists the possibility of over-teaching, of focusing too much on the drills or placing too much emphasis on practice.

Perhaps no content area provides better evidence of the strength of "The game is the best teacher" than that of second languages. Can there be any doubt that immersion offers the ultimate second-language learning experience? Second-language teachers know that second-language students benefit from vocabulary exercises, conjugation charts, and grammar lessons. These same teachers know, however, that no second-language instruction can do for a student what an immersion experience can. Just like with the game of soccer, the real-life experience of immersion forces a student to draw on what he's learned while simultaneously being creative and solving linguistic challenges. Such challenges simply can't be reproduced in a classroom setting, with a workbook, or even with the best second-language instructional software.

Teachers in content areas besides second languages also can approach learning with this philosophy in mind. Project-based learning for younger students provides opportunities to learn by doing. For example, a student will learn far more about the delicacy of a wetland ecosystem by actually visiting a wetland ecosystem, observing, and collecting data than she ever would by reading about such an ecosystem in a textbook or even by watching a video online. Likewise, a pre-med student spending a week as an intern in an ER or doctor's office can and will learn things that simply can't be replicated even in the best college or university. Teacher-education programs use this approach, too, when education students must complete student-teaching before they receive a diploma or certification. After all, what college professor could accurately simulate your first day in your own classroom?

Whether the instructor coaches soccer or teaches Mandarin Chinese, only so much education and preparation can happen on a practice field or in a classroom. Valuable direct instruction, combined with world-class drills and exercises, offers only so much benefit for students. Players and students alike need coaches and teachers to prepare them up to a point. However, after a student receives top-notch coaching and instruction, there simply can be no substitute for real-life situations when it comes to the best and most meaningful student learning. Coaches and teachers can be good, or even great, but in soccer as well as in many, many other disciplines the game is the best teacher.

6

The Power of Creative Play

> **“**Creativity is as important now in education as literacy and we should treat it with the same status.**”**
>
> (Sir Ken Robinson)

When looking for one of the most respected high school football coaches in America, one might not think to look at a prestigious private school like Phillips Andover Academy. Often referred to simply as Andover, the elite private school in Massachusetts boasts an impressive list of grads including Samuel Morse, Humphrey Bogart, George Bush, George W. Bush, H.G. Bissinger (author of *Friday Night Lights*), and a host of winners of such awards as the Nobel Prize and the Pulitzer Prize. However, during the mid-twentieth century, one of the nation's most esteemed high school football coaches, Steve Sorota, devoted more than four decades to coaching and teaching young men at Andover. Interestingly, one of Sorota's former players at Andover, Bill Belichick, went on to spend nearly four decades as a coach in the NFL, where he has collected three Super Bowl victories. Sorota had multiple opportunities to leave Andover during his tenure at Andover, but he remained loyal to the school and dedicated to his players. What could have made Sorota so content at Andover that he always turned down offers from larger schools and even colleges?

As a young coach, Steve Sorota benefited greatly from the wisdom and vision of Andover's then-headmaster, Claude Moore Fuess. When Fuess hired Sorota, Fuess made clear his priorities for the new coach: teaching first, and winning football games second. Fuess explained that Sorota would be evaluated not on wins and losses but rather on the effect his teaching had on the young men in the football program. Sorota couldn't have been more thrilled and Andover proved a great fit for the youngster.

Sorota coached his players hard and taught them the tough, physical game of football. After all, he had learned from one of the best and toughest coaches ever, Vince Lombardi, at Fordham University. Sorota prepared his players thoroughly, often approached the game as a science, and even pioneered the practice of mandatory study of game film. However, with no pressure from his administration to win, with no pressure to reach arbitrary benchmarks, Sorota experimented and allowed his players to experiment. Sorota tried new things. Sorota encouraged his players to be creative and to problem-solve on their own without having to fear potential repercussions for mistakes or losses. Sorota believed so much in this model of learning that he began practices with "sandbox" time, during which he required players to "horse around" and explore the game of football.

Sorota, because of the way he taught, felt the freedom during games to allow his players to work things out for themselves, to call their own plays, and to experience both successes and failures. Unlike so many coaches, he had no fear of mistakes and his players adopted that mindset, too. Where else but in a game would players really develop and progress? How else but through trial and error would players learn? For Sorota, such an approach seemed the only appropriate one for allowing his players to grow and mature. For Sorota, that was education. Perhaps Sorota would have agreed that the game is the best teacher.

Sorota's story is compelling because there are two valuable lessons here for educators. The first comes not from Sorota but from his headmaster, Claude Moore Fuess. The wise headmaster emphasized teaching and learning more than winning and freed Sorota to do what he did best: just teach. And Sorota did just that, in his own creative way. Sorota, who valued the autonomy and the trust, responded to the challenge by remaining loyal to Andover for more than 40 years and by winning more than his fair share of football games.

A classroom environment mirroring Sorota's experience at Andover would be a dream come true for students and teachers alike. Imagine a teaching environment in which teaching and learning are emphasized more than scores and test results. Imagine a learning environment in which students are allowed to experiment and make mistakes without the fear or pressure of high-stakes, punitive consequences. Imagine a teaching environment in which teachers are given autonomy and freedom to explore with students, to be spontaneous, and to allow students to do their own creative exploration. Such a learning environment allows for authentic, meaningful teaching and learning.

The second lesson comes from Sorota's commitment to his players' creative exploration of the game of football, both during "sandbox" time and during games. Sorota valued exploratory play for what it could teach his players and for the problem-solving skills it developed. From infancy through adulthood, human beings simply are wired to learn through play. Infants and young children learn about their environment and their own bodies, about socialization and language, and about cause and effect, all through play. Elementary students learn math skills through creative play with manipulatives. Middle and high school students learn science through hands-on experimentation and exploration in labs, artistic techniques through creative work in multiple media, and technology skills through "playing around" with software and hardware – when done correctly, all forms of play. Play and creative exploration, when incorporated into almost any discipline or topic, add an element of fun, increase engagement, and encourage curiosity. Effective teachers strive for each of these in the classroom. While teaching and coaching remain vital to student development, the significance of play and creative exploration cannot be overstated. Environments in which this type of learning are both allowed and fostered will be far more conducive to teaching and learning, and, ultimately, to student success. Sorota and Fuess knew this, and classroom teachers would do well to follow their lead.

7

Adding a Level of Competition

" Winning is important to me, but what brings
me real joy is the experience of
being fully engaged in whatever I'm doing. **"**

(Phil Jackson, 11-time NBA champion as
a head coach with the Chicago Bulls
and Los Angeles Lakers)

For as long as man has been running and wrestling and hurling objects through the air, he has been in competition. Competition lies at the heart of all sports. Whether individuals compete against one another, teams compete against teams, or individuals compete against themselves, sport centers on competition. Spectators and fans love competition and competition is the reason professional coaches and athletes have jobs in the first place. Private coaches and trainers stay employed because individuals like to compete against themselves, against others, against a course, or against nature. As with all things, too much competition or too much emphasis on competition can be unhealthy. When managed and used as a coaching tool, though, competition can provide very healthy stimulus and motivation, it can heighten focus and concentration, and it can equip people with, well, a competitive edge.

Because competition lies at the heart of all that coaches and players strive to accomplish, competition, and specifically winning or excelling in competition, tends to be seen as the end goal of coaching and training. Great coaches, though, use competition not just as the end but often as part of their training, teaching, and practicing regimens. Great coaches, like all-time winningest US high school soccer coach *Terry Michler* and 22-time women's soccer NCAA champion coach *Anson Dorrance,* make competition an integral part of practice. Much of the work they do in practice every day involves competition not only between individual players but also between groups of players. *Patti Gerckens,* coach of the 2011 UC San Diego national championship softball team, also relies heavily on integrating competition into her practices. Gerckens says, "Competition breeds success and that is how we get better. We can't be afraid to push each other and, in fact, it is expected." Gerckens hit the nail on the head about pushing one another through competition. Individuals, groups, and teams improve when they push themselves and one another to work harder, perform at a higher level, and reach new heights. Therein lies the beauty of competition.

Professional athletes and elite NCAA athletes aren't the only people who enjoy competition. In fact, people of all ages love competition, and especially kids. Even a casual observer of an elementary school playground will see children naturally competing in all sorts of activities: running, climbing across monkey bars, kicking a ball, or jumping rope. A great teacher, regardless of the age of student she teaches, can infuse competition occasionally to energize a class, challenge her students, raise the level of achievement or performance, and encourage students to work even harder. In a word, a great teacher can increase engagement through competition.

Competition in the classroom need not be a high-stakes, winner-take-all, cut-throat game where winners are glorified and losers are scorned. Rather, competition in the classroom can be just plain fun. The goal for a great teacher using competition in the classroom is finding a healthy, enjoyable amount of developmentally appropriate competition. Reviewing for tests can be great fun and highly engaging when couched as a competitive game. Drilling math facts, vocabulary, and spelling words can be competitive. Competition can take math or grammar board work to a new level. Economics students using a stock-market game can compete against one another, other groups, other classes, or even against the teacher. Competition in the classroom doesn't always have to be about the fastest, the smartest, or the most right answers, either. Competition in the classroom can focus on all sorts of interesting things like creativity, effort, neatness, attention to detail, or being encouraging.

Much of the work Michler, Dorrance, Gerckens, and other great coaches require of their players would become mundane and monotonous without competition. If the coaches simply sent players to separate areas of the field to work on drills and skill development, they largely would fail to keep the players fully engaged. When players aren't fully engaged, they likely won't work as hard as they might otherwise would or as long as they should. By making some of the work competitive, these coaches engage their players. The work becomes more meaningful and, with the introduction of a social component, the work becomes more fun. When competing, even in simple games or tasks that are not high-stakes, players work harder and work to come through for their teammates, their peers. These same concepts transfer easily to a great teacher's classroom. Mundane work can be transformed into fun, meaningful practice by adding a little competition to the mix. Using competition in the classroom also adds a social component to learning and students of all ages love being social.

In official, sanctioned games and matches, winners usually earn a "win," a prize, a trophy, or something else tangible or quantifiable. In unofficial competitions, such as those that take place regularly on practice fields or in classrooms, winners don't always have to earn a prize or avoid some negative consequence for winning. In unofficial "practice" competitions, coaches and teachers alike have numerous opportunities to teach lessons about intrinsic motivation, about winning for the sake of winning, about being satisfied with a job well done, and about working hard for the benefit of classmates or teammates. The practice time and classroom time also provide coaches and teachers with opportunities to teach little lessons before, during, and after competition about winning and losing, as well as about grit and effort. After all, great coaches and teachers seize opportunities through sports and with classroom experiences to teach young people about life. As competition always will be part of life, great coaches and teachers can infuse competition into their teaching not only to increase student engagement but also to teach valuable life lessons.

8

Keeping it Real

❝Game situation as much as possible! If the players can
relate a drill to a part of the game it is easier
for them to translate and work hard during a drill.❞

(*Terry Schroeder*, coach of Pepperdine University
men's water polo, NCAA national champion,
and Olympic medalist as athlete and coach)

"When am I actually going to use this?" Perhaps every teacher dating as far back as Socrates has heard this or some variation of this question. Similarly, most coaches have heard some variation of this question, too. Great teachers and coaches alike have been and always will be ready to answer this question, regardless of what lesson or skill the students or players tackle. In the sports world, a great coach knows that one of the keys to successful, meaningful practice is making as many drills and activities as possible correlate directly to game situations. In other words, each drill, each movement, each touch on the ball should have meaning in the context of an actual game situation. Without such context, what value does the drill or activity hold? If a drill has no correlation to a real-game situation, how else might the players' time and energy be better spent? As long as a drill or activity has a correlation to a real-game situation, though, a coach can be ready to answer a player's question about when he is going to use this.

When a great coach executes a practice plan with a real-game situation in mind, he works hard to make the practice as game-like as possible, often including either the complexity or speed of an actual game. After all, if a practice activity does not simulate a game, how can players be ready for a real game? If a practice activity does not simulate a game, how can a player successfully transfer skills from practice to a real game? Hall of Fame volleyball coach Marv Dunphy follows this line of thinking even with the elite athletes he coaches at Pepperdine University. Dunphy says, "The hardest thing we have to do as coaches is get them to train at a level they have to in order to be good. I like to practice at game speed and train to reality. You want it to be as game-like as possible. How much transfer do you want from practice to the game? You want 100 percent." Like other great coaches, he trains to reality, or practices in situations that simulate real games as often as possible.

Great teachers, like great coaches, train to reality. Especially as we navigate further into the twenty-first century, classroom learning must become more and more real-world if classrooms are to prepare students for life beyond the classroom walls. Necessarily, activities designed for students should become increasingly real-world, with a direct correlation to real-world situations. While the execution of this idea varies with the age of the students and the lessons being taught, training to reality simply makes sense in today's classrooms. Great teachers who train to reality, who take whatever they're doing and teaching and correlate it directly to some real-world situation, give their students a monumental advantage over students who do not benefit from similar teaching. Math problems, grammar and vocabulary lessons, equations, current events, lab reports, and even research papers done in isolation can leave students feeling like the work they're doing is not real-world but rather just busy-work or school-work. Each of these examples can be made, with a little work and some creativity, to simulate real-world situations. Great teachers transition students from thinking in terms of school-work to thinking in terms of life-work. This only happens, though, when a great teacher trains to reality.

As they always have and always will, students want to know how they will use in the real world anything and everything they're asked to do. As long as a teacher frequently and consistently simulates the real world, or trains to reality, she'll always be able to answer those questions. For younger students, the answer may be, "You'll need these facts to do fractions in third grade," or "You'll use these sentences to write whole paragraphs and whole stories next year." For middle-grade students, teachers may say, "The chemistry basics you're learning here will be helpful not only in high school science courses but also in handling various household chemicals at your house," or "The oral communication skills we're practicing now will help you when you interview for a job or for college admissions several years from now." To high school students, a teacher might say, "You'll need these time management skills to plan your days and weeks wisely in college," or "This calculus will be important for engineering courses as well as for finance and business courses you may encounter in college." Additionally, by simulating the real world and pointing out to her students how their learning in the classroom connects to the outside world, a great teacher can do something transformational: she can empower her students to begin looking at the world differently, to see math, science, etc., all around them in the real world. Just as Marv Dunphy and other great coaches train their athletes to reality and make practices as game-like, or real-world, as possible, a great teacher trains her students to reality, or prepares them for the real world, by creating situations in the classroom that mirror the real world. There really can be no better training in the classroom than the proper equipping of students for life outside it.

Section IV

Embrace Technology

1

Meet Them Where They Are

“ We communicate visually as much as possible –
so many of our players are visual learners.
With so much visual stimulation in their lives,
the old chalk board or dry erase board just does
not cut it anymore. We look to integrate websites
and video clips whenever possible.
Smartphones, iPads, and laptops on the practice
field can greatly enhance the learning process,
especially if we are introducing something brand new. **”**

(*Tom O'Grady*, former US Lacrosse Man of the Year
and three-time US Lacrosse Coach of the Year)

One of the fundamental concepts of both coaching and teaching is this: meet the learner where he is and then help him move forward. One could interpret this in a number of ways. Meet the learner where he is in terms of his knowledge, for example, or his skill level, his level of comprehension, his level of motivation, and more. The football coaching staff at Dowling Catholic High School in West Des Moines, Iowa, provide a great example of yet another interpretation: meet the learner where he is technologically. Under the direction of head coach *Tom Wilson*, Dowling Catholic High School has advanced to the

4A state football finals five times, capturing the state championship in 2010 and 2013. Certainly great coaching and teaching combined with outstanding effort from the Dowling Catholic athletes factor heavily in the program's success. As Wilson and *Kurt Zimmerman*, Dowling Catholic's assistant coach and IT guru, attest, clever use of technology certainly has played a role in the success of recent years.

Wilson and his staff work to teach their visual learners in such a way that they learn best. For example, in the preseason, much of the instruction occurs the way the players' math, science, or English instruction does. "Our athletes are visual in their learning," says Wilson. "Our preseason meetings are done in the classroom setting. This allows us to put our students in a visual learning environment then take what they learned directly to the practice field for implementation." Part of what they do initially in the classroom involves using software like Hudl. "Hudl allows us to visually teach our athletes through video," adds Wilson. Wilson and his staff recognize that their players are visual learners so they take very deliberate steps to meet them where they are in terms of learning visually. For Dowling Catholic, though, there's more to the story.

Assistant Coach Kurt Zimmerman brings to the Dowling Catholic coaching staff not only 15 years of coaching experience but also, and perhaps equally as important, 20 years' experience in IT. That unique combination of experiences gives Zimmerman a unique perspective on twenty-first-century learners and how technology can be incorporated into the teaching plan for them. Zimmerman observes of twenty-first-century learners, "Their lives revolve around technology – smart phones, video game consoles, tablet computers, smart cars – the list goes on and on. This also is a generation that is very much used to information coming at them not only at lightning speed, but in very small, concise snippets (tweets, texts, etc.). They expect to get answers quickly and to not have to spend much time on a subject, otherwise they lose interest. Most of the content that our youth see is also multimedia focused, allowing them to get at information much differently than we [today's adults] did in plain old text."

In terms of meeting learners where they are technologically, Zimmerman empowers the rest of the coaching staff to be able to provide football instruction that mirrors the way twenty-first-century learners communicate and receive information. "Technologies, especially tools like Hudl, have given us the ability to apply the concepts of short bits of focused information in a multi-media format to help train our athletes. Rather than sit through hours of film review to get at a dozen key plays or points of emphasis, we are able to pull those dozen together and focus on them for teaching. While techniques like drawing plays on a white board still have value, we are now able to enhance that by pulling up clips that show the actual execution of the play." Rather than gripe or fuss about how kids have changed over the years, the Dowling Catholic staff have embraced the changes in today's learners and have embraced the technology that allows them to better provide instruction for their players.

Wilson and Zimmerman have found another powerful way to use technology to literally meet their learners where they are. Much the way the flipped classroom model of learning makes instruction available to students anytime and anywhere they have access to Internet and a device, Dowling Catholic football coaches use similar technology to push information out to their players digitally. Providing information and some instruction digitally for their players has allowed the players to become learners from home, on a bus, on vacation, or anywhere else they happen to be as long as they have Internet and a device. Providing information and instruction digitally also allows learners to schedule their own learning outside of the classroom or athletic field. As twenty-first-century kids become busier and busier, flexible learning times outside the traditional instructional times and locations will continue to grow in importance. Describing their experience with flipping football instruction, Zimmerman explains: "By having content available over the Internet, we are able to push training out to our athletes at any time, allowing the athlete to be able to access it over and over when it works in their busy lives. I know this [technology] has helped smaller programs be able to provide feedback that they may not have been able to provide in the past." Citing an example from a small community in northern Minnesota, Zimmerman says: "In the past, due to the distance from town for many of the athletes, and the difficulty in asking them to come in [for practice or instruction] outside of normal school days, not much review and preparation was done off the field. Now that they are using Hudl, the coaches are able to push out coaching to the athletes, and use telestrating and voice-over tools to coach the kids up remotely – very powerful." With such success in West Des Moines as evidence, the Dowling Catholic High School football players certainly seem to have responded to the football staff's efforts to use technology to meet the players where they are, not only figuratively but also literally.

Classroom teachers everywhere, like the coaching staff at Dowling Catholic High School, face a shifting instructional landscape in the twenty-first century. As Kurt Zimmerman points out, today's learners have never known a time when they haven't been completely immersed and bombarded with technology. Today's learners, astutely named "Digital Natives" by researcher Marc Prensky, actually learn differently than students even a generation ago, arguably because of the way they've been immersed in media and technology their entire lives. Technology may not be the only means by which teachers will effectively reach twenty-first-century learners, but it will play a role. Great teachers of the twenty-first century will be those who, like Wilson and Zimmerman, embrace not only the changes in learners and learning but also in teaching and technology's role in the craft.

Dowling Catholic's model of embracing technology and integrating it into their football instruction provides a fantastic model for great teachers of the twenty-first century. First, educational technology offers a powerful, effective way to meet today's students where they are in terms of interest and relevance. Because so many facets of students' lives are centered on and affected by technology, they respond to technology and engage quickly with digital content. Great teachers should be ecstatic at this news because technology can be such an effective tool for getting students to engage in virtually any subject, any topic, any time, any place. Furthermore, technology often can make even the most mundane topics and concepts more relevant and twenty-first-century. This is true for first-grade math facts, a fourth-grade unit on prepositions, a middle school grammar lesson, or a high school unit on supply and demand. Just as no technology ever could replace the great coaches at Dowling Catholic, even the latest and greatest technology won't replace great teachers; teachers should avoid Luddite mentalities and rest a little easier at this news.

As European Tour coach and Fellow of the PGA golf coach *Hugh Marr* says, "Technological advances mean that any of these tools become more crucial to good coaching, always under the proviso that technology never can take over! Great coaching has been and always will be about dealing with human beings on their terms." Marr's idea directly correlates to teachers and teaching. Great teachers, though, can leverage the benefits of technology to meet students at the intersection of the high-tech, multi-media and their lives.

Educational technology, secondly, offers an avenue for great teachers to meet students where they are literally, physically, and geographically. Whether teachers flip their classrooms and post lectures online, post homework online for students to work remotely, or connect students to engaging enrichment material online, time and geography no longer stand as obstacles for great teachers. Great teachers can generate or link to powerful, media-rich content for students to access from practically any device with Internet access. Busy students can access such content whenever and wherever best works for them. They can watch video, pause, rewind, and watch again as much and as often as they need. They can participate in conversations – both text based, as with a blog or chat, and virtually, as with Skype or FaceTime – in real time with anyone almost anywhere in the world. Students can work practice problems, complete assessments, and turn in homework with instant results, again, from anywhere they can access the Internet on their devices. Great teachers can shift some of the teaching and learning outside the traditional classroom hours and locales so that different learning experiences can happen in the classrooms. Great teachers can share great instruction and great information not only with their students but also with students at other schools or in remote locations anywhere in the world.

As with the great staff at Dowling Catholic, the things great teachers can do now and in the future with technology are limited only by creativity and connectivity. Most schools and school districts have technology integration specialists, technology coordinators, or similar personnel who would love nothing more than to get coaches and teachers plugged in and up to speed. Teachers who don't have immediate access to educational technology specialists need only open a web browser for instant access to terabytes of information about how to get started with educational technology. There exist online count-less blogs, websites, YouTube, Vimeo, and TeacherTube videos, Twitter and Facebook users, and more, all of which are potential resources for harnessing the incredible power of technology to enhance both teaching and learning. The Dowling Catholic High School football teams have responded in grand fashion. It's pretty safe to say that math, science, reading, art, second-language, social studies, economics, and other students of all ages will respond in kind to the infusion of technology into their learning experiences.

2

Flipping Classrooms and Football Fields

> "One of the greatest benefits of flipping is that overall interaction increases: teacher-to-student, and student-to-student."
>
> (Jonathan Bergmann, author of *Flip Your Classroom: Reach Every Student in Every Class Every Day*)

What do two chemistry teachers from Colorado, Jonathan Bergmann and Aaron Sams, have in common with a high school football offensive coordinator, *Kurt Earl*, from Nebraska? They have in common the flipped classroom model of teaching. A number of years ago, Bergmann and Sams decided to try something a little unusual with their chemistry classrooms. They recorded themselves giving chemistry lectures and posted the videos on YouTube. Their chemistry students watched the direct-instruction lectures at home, on their own time, so they could focus on solving problems, doing labs, and completing assignments with their teachers, Bergmann and Sams, present and available for assistance. In other words, they flipped their classrooms. The duo eventually documented their flipping journey in a book, *Flip Your Classroom: Reach Every Student in Every Class Every Day*, which serves as a handbook for teachers who want to flip their classrooms. But what about the football coach from Nebraska?

Like Bergmann and Sams, Kurt Earl decided to flip his classroom, but Earl's classroom is a football field. Whether in the classroom or on the football field, good teaching is good teaching. Like Bergmann and Sams, Kurt Earl knows good teaching. Coach Earl, Hudl guru and offensive coordinator at Lincoln Christian School, explains his unconventional approach to teaching offensive aspects of the game of football. "Essentially, I've flipped the classroom . . . errrr . . . field. I teach concepts and big picture stuff via Hudl and teach techniques and details in person. It's more efficient and more effective. We have loads of talent, but I think our success has been, at least in part, due to the ways in which we are using Hudl to speed up the learning process." In other words, Earl teaches the *what* via recorded instruction on Hudl and teaches the *how* in person during practice.

Just as YouTube, Vimeo, TeacherTube, and other video-hosting sites offer a quick, easy, and free opportunity for teachers, or anyone else, to upload content for others to view online, Hudl provides a service specifically for coaches of any sport to upload and edit video online. As Hudl says on its website, hudl.com, until Hudl came along coaches spent lots of time converting game film to DVD. Hudl's designers wanted to make the game-film process easier and more accessible. "There was an obvious and straightforward way to help these teams: make all of the video, play diagrams, and coaching presentations securely available to the entire team over the Internet," explains the Hudl website.

Using Hudl, Coach Earl decided to flip his football instruction much the way Bergmann, Sams, and many other teachers have flipped their classrooms. Says Earl, "The ability to share video privately with the team has completely changed the way in which I install our offense. This summer before our team camps I filmed myself teaching our offense on a white board (a couple dozen three–five-minute clips) and shared them via Hudl with the coaches and players. On the first day of camp we did primarily individual work, but I told the kids to come the next day having watched the video on formations . . ." On day two, rather than teach the nuts and bolts of the offense during practice time as he had in the days before Hudl, Earl instructed a group of his players to jump right into the formations they learned via

Hudl. He made a few tiny adjustments, then sent another group in, then another, and so on. "We installed *every* detail of *all* our formations in about 10 minutes of practice time," says Earl. "Before Hudl that process took 30–45 minutes."

Earl provides information for his players outside of practice that he otherwise would have presented to them via direct instruction. By giving his players the chance to watch the video on their own time outside practice, Earl empowers his players to come to practice ready to apply the knowledge-level information they learned from the video. This plan cut instructional time significantly, thus making practice time much more efficient and more meaningful. Where Earl may have had to repeat his instruction multiple times at practice in the past, the players now have the opportunity to play and replay the videos as many times as necessary to pick up the information, thus allowing Earl to spend more practice time on application. Furthermore, his players can watch the online content on computers, tablets, and mobile devices, which makes it convenient for his players to learn on their own time both when and where they choose to engage.

Taking the flipped learning a step further, Earl now uses Hudl to prepare his players for the upcoming week of practices. "Using Hudl's playbook feature I am also able to share play diagrams and video of plays from games. I have used this in two ways. The first, and obvious, way is to simply share video for kids to watch with the diagram right there for them to view. The second way is to create diagrams of upcoming opponents' defensive alignments and share video of them playing against us last year or against opponents with similar offenses. It's our version of the scouting report. So by the time our kids get to school Monday they already know quite a bit about the upcoming opponent. When it comes time for starting offense vs. scout defense in practice, I don't teach much about the defense. We just line up and start running plays and fine tuning the details." By preparing his players for the week ahead, Earl has discovered a quick, easy, and effective way to make his practice time more meaningful and efficient. His players go to practice each Monday ready to apply the new information they learned via Hudl over the weekend.

Earl's innovative approach to football instruction perfectly illustrates the flipped classroom/flipped learning model. The official flipped classroom website, flippedlearning.org, says: "Flipped Learning occurs when direct instruction is moved from the group teaching space to the individual environment. Class time is then used for higher order, active problem solving by students and one-to-one or small group interactions with the teacher." Earl moves much of his direct instruction from the group teaching space of the football practice field to the individual environment where each player can watch when and how he wants. Earl then uses practice time for higher-order, active problem solving by asking his players to run through formations based on what they learned via Hudl. Specifically, Earl does this in small groups of 11 players at a time that easily can interact with him, the teacher. As an added bonus, this small-group work and personal interaction contributes not only to team chemistry but also to the relationship building between Earl and his players.

Can good coaching occur without using Hudl? Of course, but when used correctly Hudl provides coaches with very useful tools that certainly can make the processes of both teaching and learning more efficient and engaging, thereby making good coaches even better. Likewise, can good teaching occur without the flipped classroom model? Sure. The flipped classroom model, though, creates opportunities for good teachers to do new, different, or more things in the classroom for which a traditional teaching model does not allow.

In the traditional model of classroom instruction, the teacher often provides instruction during class and asks students to work through practice problems outside of class on their own. As students will tell you, they most need the teacher during the practice problems, not at the time of instruction. The flipped learning/flipped classroom model allows teachers to shift direct instruction and the presentation of basic facts and concepts outside the classroom so students have access to their teachers when they need them most. If students have questions or need clarification on concepts during the video instruction, they either can rewind and re-watch the teacher again and again, or come to class the next day with their questions. As students work through practice problems in class, work on projects, or do labs, the students have ready access to the teacher.

A flipped classroom allows for greater collaborative learning among students since the students are engaged in active learning and skills practice at the same time and in the same place. By moving the instruction out of the classroom, a good teacher can design and implement more collaborative learning activities than a traditional model of teaching allows because entire class periods can be devoted to hands-on, engaging, and meaningful collaborative work. The increased collaboration, made possible in part by flipping, equips students with better social skills, relationship skills, and teamwork skills, regardless of their ages. Furthermore, a good teacher can use flipping to allow for greater interaction and relationship building between him and his students.

Just as a good coach from virtually any sport can use Hudl for improving team and individual performance in a revolutionary new way, a good teacher can improve class and student learning using online video services such as YouTube, Vimeo, and TeacherTube as part of the flipped classroom model. Over the last few years, research has begun to emerge on flipping. The early research indicates what Earl has observed with his football team and what Bergmann and Sams observed with their chemistry classes: flipping the classroom can increase engagement, efficiency, and learning. It should be noted, though, that flipping never was intended to replace good teaching or good teachers, just as flipping in the sports world never can replace good coaches or coaching. Bergmann and Sams will be the first to say that, and in fact they did in their book. Rather, the flipped classroom model serves as a highly effective tool – and only a tool – for good coaches and teachers alike. What Kurt Earl says of his new model of football instruction easily could be echoed by thousands and thousands of teachers of all subjects and grade levels: "The *what* is now taught through Hudl and can be consumed on the athlete's time, which has freed up practice time to work on the *how*. That's no small thing. In fact, it's revolutionary!"

3

"There's an app for that"

" The iPod completely changed
the way people approach music. **"**

(Karl Lagerfeld)

In 2008, Apple opened the App Store for its iOS devices and forever changed the way the world looks at phones, computers, and tablets. Shortly thereafter, Apple launched a brilliant advertising campaign centered on the now-trademarked phrase, "There's an app for that." The point of the advertising campaign? Name anything you want to do with an iOS device and there is an app (software application) to help you do it or to do it for you. Interestingly, there were fewer than 100,000 apps available when the campaign started. Today consumers can download over 1,000,000 apps from the App Store, with about half of those native to iPad! This astounding number doesn't reflect the number also available for Windows, Android, and other operating system devices. It seemed true a few years ago, but truly there exists an app for pretty much anything a person might want to do with a device.

The sports world has benefited from apps considerably in the last few years. Fans can use apps to read the latest news, scores, and updates on any and every team out there. Fans can watch highlights or even stream entire games and matches using apps on their devices.

Fans can connect with coaches and athletes via Twitter, Facebook, and other social media apps, as well as through apps designed specifically by and for teams and their communities of support. In terms of productivity in the sports world, coaches have reaped the benefits of the app craze because savvy companies have hired numerous programmers to write and create apps specifically for coaches.

The list of apps available to coaches would fill an entire book and more apps become available every week. For the sake of this discussion, though, here are just a few of the myriad apps available for tech-savvy coaches. Coaches who want to enhance their use of video for practices, for one-on-one sessions, or for team teaching can check out apps like Coach's Eye and Ubersense Coach. Coach's Eye makes it easy for a coach to break down video of a pitching motion, a volleyball serve, a golf swing, or even a swim stroke, and provide instant feedback for athletes using the video. Ubersense Coach, using imported video, allows a coach to use slow-motion video analysis, on-screen drawing tools, as well as side-by-side and overlay views to provide invaluable feedback to athletes. Golf GPS and similar apps give golfers, caddies, and coaches crazy amounts of data about virtually any golf course by using GPS to give distances to hazards, bunkers, greens, and flagsticks. Volleyball coaches can use Coach's Clipboard, Assistant Coach Volleyball, Volleyball Lineup Tracker, and other apps to manage practice and game stats, lineups and rotations, drills, and more. Gamechanger Scorekeeping enables baseball, softball, and basketball coaches to track and manage all kinds of game stats electronically. The list simply goes on and on.

Why do more coaching apps appear in the app stores for the various operating systems every week? Savvy coaches have embraced technology. Coaches who have embraced technology have done so not to replace anything they do as coaches, but rather as a tool to make tasks more effective, more efficient, or more beneficial for the players in terms of learning. Is there a learning curve for using an app to track stats instead of paper and pencil, for example? Perhaps, but the statistics recorded electronically become much more robust, searchable, and sortable than ever before, thus empowering the coach to make data-based decisions and to teach more efficiently than ever. What coach wouldn't want that?

When it comes to embracing technology as a teaching tool, some coaches have set the bar pretty high for their counterparts in the classroom. The exciting news is that the number of educational apps available for teachers far exceeds the number available for coaches. Truly, there probably is an app available for virtually any grade level, any subject, any operating system, and any budget. Interested in math apps? Take a look at the incredibly powerful Wolfram Alpha, which gives users access to the powerful "computational knowledge engine"; Algebra Solver, which solves formulas and equations and allows the user to email solutions; iFormulas, which allows the user to look up mathematical formulas; Appolonius, which allows the user to create fascinating geometric structures; Doodle Numbers, which uses games to challenge the user and build math skills; and Math Evolve, which also uses games to help the user develop number sense, math skills, and more. If science is your subject, consider the NASA App, which connects the user to news, updates, feature stories, video, astronaut Tweets, and more; The Elements, which offers a fascinating new look at nature's building blocks; Science 360, the National Science Foundation's app which connects the user to incredible images, video, and stories from the science world; Moon Globe HD, which gives the user some stunning perspectives of earth's natural satellite; or 3D Brain, which gives the user an interactive tour of all the regions and structures of the human brain. Looking for social studies apps? Try the MyCongress app, which gives the user access to loads of data about Congress, news, video, tweets from Congressmen, and more, or Barefoot World Atlas, which is a stunning, interactive 3D globe. There's plenty for English and language arts teachers, too, including I Tell a Story, which allows the user to record his voice to narrate a story; Story Kit, which allows the user to create an electronic storybook; Story Builder, which helps the user with paragraph formation and idea integration; and Sentencebuilder, which helps the younger user with grammar and writing.

For nearly any activity a teacher does in the classroom, someone probably has designed an app to make that activity easier, faster, better, or more engaging. Additionally, many apps make classroom activities possible that never even existed a decade ago, a year ago, or even a month ago. If a teacher wants an app for her own device or computer, it's probably out there. If a teacher wants an app for student devices or computers, it's also probably out there. A savvy teacher needs only to do a little "legwork" to find just the right app. For starters, a teacher can probably contact someone in the instructional technology department of the school or district. A quick conversation with an IT specialist can help the specialist find exactly what the teacher needs. Likewise, if a teacher isn't sure what she needs, an IT specialist may be able to recommend a few to try and even provide several for the teacher to experiment with at home or in the classroom.

For the teacher who wants to just jump right in, finding just the right app could be just a few clicks away. A simple search of the app store for the teacher's device or operating system is a great way to start looking for apps. A search using keywords like *chemistry*, *elements*, *periodic table*, or the like, should produce a nice list of apps to browse and consider. The same goes for keywords from any content area, as well as any task like *grading*, *student response system*, etc. To help take some of the mystery out of app, purchases, most app stores give consumers information about each app, including how often it's been downloaded, customer reviews and ratings, intended age of user, and more.

With the availability and ease of use of apps for the classroom, teachers in the twenty-first century really have no excuse for not exploring apps other than, perhaps, "I have neither a device nor a computer." In all other cases, these engaging, powerful applications are there for the taking and more join the ranks often. Because many, many of the educational apps have been designed by teachers or with input from teachers, it doesn't take long to find apps that actually are useful. Three other points worth mentioning about many of these apps . . . they're cool and they're fun and kids love them! Take a look at the app store for your device or operating system. Chances are that you will be blown away.

4 — Immediate Data Yields Immediate Feedback

66 Feedback is the breakfast of champions.**99**

(Ken Blanchard)

Technology has revolutionized both teaching and learning. Technology has changed how, when, and where content and instruction can be delivered and consumed. Technology has allowed for student engagement at unprecedented levels. Technology has provided opportunities for teachers and students to have real-time conversations and interactions with others down the hall and around the globe. Practically no facet of either teaching or learning remains unaffected by technology. With all the glitz and glamour of the hardware, content, and communications, though, the revolutionary assessment and feedback methods forever changed by technology occasionally get overlooked.

Learners must receive meaningful feedback from teachers, both in the classroom and on the field, if they are to grow and develop properly. Just as math students or second-language students need feedback on their work, athletes need feedback on their footwork, their swing, their routes, and other skills. Great teachers and coaches know the importance of providing feedback as quickly as possible after a student works a problem or takes a swing. The sooner a learner receives feedback, the sooner he either can move on to the next concept or skill, or the sooner he can correct his issue and try once more to demonstrate mastery of the concept or skill. The farther removed from an action the feedback is provided, the less meaningful and impactful the feedback will be. Therefore, when it comes to providing feedback to help a student or a player master a concept or skill, a great teacher desires nothing more than to be able to provide that feedback quickly.

In terms of teaching and instruction, technology has revolutionized the game of golf perhaps more than any other. With the advent of slow-motion video and replay, golf instructors and coaches enjoyed the ability to record a player's swing and examine every aspect of the swing that never could have happened with the naked eye. Now, however, with technology like Trackman and FlightScope, a golf instructor can collect insane amounts of data and provide meaningful feedback to the golf student literally as soon as the player finishes his swing. These incredible systems use advanced technology to measure and predict, almost unbelievably, things like club speed, attack angle, club path, swing plane, ball speed, launch angle, launch direction, spin axis, spin rate, height, carry, landing angle, and more. With data like that at one's disposal almost instantly, a golf instructor like Hugh Marr can correct even the tiniest issues with a golfer's swing literally between swings. Additionally, a golf instructor can record a golfer's swing data and track the data historically looking for trends and patterns.

As a golf coach on the European Tour, the UK's first accredited "Trackman Master," coach of multiple national champion golf teams at Surrey, and Head of Boys Coaching for England Golf, Hugh Marr knows more than a little about golf instruction. As good a coach as Marr was before the arrival of technology like Trackman, he will be the first to admit how much better he's become with the available technology. "I've long extolled the virtues of technology to enhance a coach's skill as a problem finder, problem solver and communicator." According to Marr, "Recent advances with radar technology such as Trackman and Flightscope have, without doubt, made me a better coach. Feedback is much more immediate, more accurate, and can be delivered and used in many different ways by both coach and athlete." Using data collected by this technology, Marr says, "I can be much more specific in how I measure success and target much more accurately the key areas for improvement. The ability to truly quantify the player's progress against these measurable goals helps develop confidence in the player, the coach and the process. Goal setting becomes more structured and specific. And, finally, the coaching process has a good deal more structure."

Football provides another great example of how technology provides coaches with an opportunity to teach using immediate feedback. Kurt Zimmerman, assistant coach and IT specialist for the Dowling Catholic High School football program, praises not only technology but also the way it allows coaches to provide instruction quickly. "Not only has technology such as Hudl helped us in the classroom setting with our athletes, but by taking advantage of devices like tablets or phones, we are able to take it [technology] on the field and record and playback in real-time. For example, if we are trying to teach a blocking technique or footwork we can record the athlete and immediately show how to correct the technique." Zimmerman goes on to say, "Imagine bringing those kinds of capabilities into the day-to-day classroom. Here's great news for teachers: there's no need to imagine . . . The technology exists for teachers to collect data and provide immediate feedback in the classroom."

In the classrooms of the twentieth century, limitations abounded for teachers who wanted to collect data and provide immediate feedback. Until very recently, there existed no real way to collect large amounts of student data, store the data, sort the data, and use the data to provide feedback in a timely manner. Pen and paper tests, quizzes, and homework needed to be graded before feedback could be provided. Even tests using Scantron or similar grading tools had to be run through a machine, grades recorded, averaged, and so on. Using the data from these assessments to look for trends and patterns required serious number crunching, another time-consuming activity. Technological advances have changed that forever.

With the boom in educational apps, educational software, and online educational options, teachers have myriad choices now for virtually any subject or grade level. Khan Academy, for example, offers a great online option in a number of subject areas for either a student or teacher looking for online instruction and assessment. A student can create an account, watch videos, and complete assessments to track his progress. The online assessment software provides instant feedback on the skills the student has mastered or the skills the student needs to practice more. If a student zips through the assessment with great accuracy, the software automatically presents only a few problems before allowing the student to advance to a more difficult skill or concept. If a student struggles on an assessment, the software gives the student more practice. A teacher can enroll an entire class, assign videos and assessments, and then can track a crazy amount of data for each student in her class for each assignment the class tackles. She can see how long each student worked on a given problem or set of problems, how many problems each answered correctly or incorrectly, what kinds of problems gave students the most difficulty, and more. Why is this so valuable? A great teacher can watch her students work and she can collect data in real time, thus allowing her to reteach the class, work with individual students on particular skills, move on to new concepts, or select additional practice work to reinforce concepts. The data from Khan Academy can be viewed instantly, stored, tracked, and sorted.

Similar work can be done in language classrooms, science classrooms, and others. Using software like Rosetta Classroom or Duolingo, students progress through language instruction in languages like Spanish, French, German, Italian, and more. In addition to the language instruction and drills, the software provides assessments that allow progress to be tracked. A great language teacher can use these or similar software to collect data instantly upon a student's completion of an exercise or assessment and then can decide how best to help each student depending upon what the data indicates. Just as Hugh Marr described the value of Trackman to golf instructors, a language instructor using this kind of software can be more specific in how she targets instruction to hit key areas of improvement, in how she measures progress, and in how she structures the teaching process. A number of states and universities offer online tests, quizzes, homework, and general assessments in a variety of math and science courses. These online assessment services also provide instant results so the teacher can provide immediate feedback or make immediate instructional adjustments.

Just as technology has revolutionized assessment for individuals and for classes, technology has changed forever standardized testing.

For example, the ERB tests that are part of the CTP, or Comprehensive Testing Program, can be taken online as of just a few years ago. These rigorous online achievement tests have been used for years by many schools to measure achievement across grades 1–11 in areas like reading, math, verbal and quantitative reasoning, science, and more. These tests have been great measures of achievement, but the results traditionally have taken weeks if not months to receive when schools used the pencil and paper versions. Once the results finally arrived back at a school, valuable instructional time had already lapsed. With the online version of these tests, school leaders and teachers have volumes of sortable data that can be used to immediately identify needs for individual students, for grade levels, for groups of students, for subject areas, and the list goes on. Having such data available as soon as the assessments are done can make as much difference for great math and reading teachers as Trackman does for Hugh Marr. When a great teacher has very specific data on the progress and skill level of each of her students, as well as all of her students collectively, she can focus her efforts to address any weaknesses or anomalies that the data reveals. Again, such data allows a great teacher to target instruction to hit key areas of improvement and add very intentional structure to the teaching process.

For teachers who prefer to create their own assessments, technology now makes that possible, too. With online options like WebAssign or Quizlet, teachers can create their own online assessments that yield instant data. The website at WebAssign says, "In brief, instructors create assignments online within WebAssign and electronically transmit them to their class. Students enter their answers online, and WebAssign automatically grades the assignment and gives students instant feedback on their performance." Similarly, Quizlet allows a teacher to create quizzes online for any subject. Quizlet also grades instantly and yields data right away to the teacher and to students. Though these are just two examples, other software options exist with an array of features.

To be sure, great teachers have been doing great work in classrooms worldwide long before the educational technology revolution exploded a few years ago. With the technology now available to them – and often available for free – great teachers have at their disposal powerful tools to enhance and improve not only teaching and learning but also assessment and feedback. As Hugh Marr, one of Europe's leading golf instructors before the technology boom in golf, readily admits, "Recent advances with radar technology . . . have, without doubt, made me a better coach. Feedback is much more immediate, more accurate, and can be delivered and used in many different ways by both coach and athlete." Marr's testimony easily could be reworded just a bit and attributed to great teachers around the world: "Recent advances with educational technology have, without doubt, made me a better teacher. Feedback is much more immediate, more accurate, and can be delivered and used in many different ways by both teacher and student." For the great teachers of the twenty-first century, this could become their mantra.

Section V

Build a Winning Tradition

1

Defining Wins and Losses

❝We define what success is to us. Success is not winning national championships, or winning all of our games. It has to be so much bigger than that . . . If success is only about winning, you are missing the boat.**❞**

(*Brad Frost*, coach of the two-time NCAA national champion University of Minnesota women's ice hockey team)

When a great coach takes the helm of an athletic team or program, he or she often addresses the team, the parents, or perhaps even the media, and promises to build a winning tradition. Once that coach establishes as a goal for the program "building a winning tradition," the first step toward reaching that goal often is defining the word *winning*. If the coach doesn't clarify exactly what winning is, how will anyone know when the program has successfully built a winning tradition? The answer may seem obvious, but the question is worth exploring further.

Generally speaking, winning in the world of athletics centers on Wins and Losses, specifically having more Wins than Losses over a given period of time. Everyone from the fanatical season ticket holders to weekend soccer moms probably would argue that a winning tradition has been established only after a coach has led his team to more

Wins than Losses. A great coach knows, though, that building a winning tradition begins long before a team notches its first Win under his or her leadership. The significance of this idea lies in the definition of winning, and just as importantly, in the definitions of Wins and Losses.

A great coach knows and understands the subtle but fundamental difference between Wins and Losses, defined as the results displayed on the scoreboard at the end of competitions, and wins and losses, defined as the multitude of smaller successes and setbacks occurring daily in practice and preparation. Fairly or unfairly, Wins and Losses will be the metric used by the public at large to determine whether the winning tradition has been delivered as promised. Therefore, fans and critics alike wait anxiously for the Wins to pile up because the public at large does not understand what a great coach knows to be true: building a winning tradition begins with wins, not with Wins. In order for the Wins to come, there must be countless wins, or small successes, first. A great coach knows that focusing solely on Wins and Losses will produce poor results. When a team focuses solely on the Wins and Losses, or the performance, outcomes, and results the public wants to see, the emphasis shifts away from the process and from building grit, resilience, determination, and mastery of skills, the very building blocks of a winning tradition.

If a coach fails to communicate clearly to his team or program not only the difference between Wins and Losses and wins and losses but also which of the two the coach values most, the team or program very easily can be caught up in chasing outcomes, thereby making the winning tradition all the more elusive. When the public at large clamors for more Wins, they usually do so without the knowledge that every day in practice and preparation the coach has placed more emphasis on wins, or smaller successes, that can be used as stepping stones than on Wins. A great coach knows not only that wins lead to Wins but also that this philosophy must be communicated to those he leads. A great coach must define winning as "experiencing small successes and getting wins first in order to get Wins later." In other words, the coach must communicate the value of the hard work that must be done, and done correctly, in order for the Wins to finally be realized.

A striking comparison can be made here between education and athletics, and between teachers and coaches. A great teacher, like a great coach, works hard to build a winning tradition with each new school year. In education, as in athletics, there exist both Wins and Losses and wins and losses, and a great teacher knows the difference. Today more than ever stakeholders and critics demand Wins from teachers and schools. While Wins in the athletic world represent outcomes reflected as points on a scoreboard, Wins in the education world represent outcomes such as state test scores, national standardized exam scores, and Advanced Placement Exam scores, to name just a few.

In light of this pressure for Wins, a great teacher holds fast to the idea that winning must be defined as "experiencing small successes and getting wins first in order to get Wins later." In order for the Wins to come in the classroom or school, there must be countless wins first. A great teacher knows that focusing solely on Wins and Losses will produce poor results. When a teacher, class, or school focuses solely on the Wins and Losses, or the outcomes and results the public wants to see, i.e. test and exam scores, the emphasis shifts away from building grit, resilience, determination, and mastery of skills, the very building blocks of a winning educational tradition. The public at large probably would argue that a winning tradition for a teacher or a school should be measured by Wins and Losses, but a great teacher knows a winning tradition must be measured by the many smaller successes experienced daily during practice and preparation. A great teacher, like a great coach, knows the Wins eventually will come, but not without wins first.

2

Getting Early Wins

" Celebrate the small successes along the way. **"**

(*Terry Schroeder*, coach of Pepperdine University men's
water polo team, NCAA national champion, and
Olympic medalist as athlete and coach)

Placing more emphasis on Wins than on wins presents an interesting logistical problem for any coach who sets out to build a winning tradition that way. No coach on the planet can lead a team to a Win before the first game, match, or competition of the season. Considering this obvious but problematic fact, can a coach realistically begin to build a winning tradition before he or she has an opportunity to officially record the first Win? The answer is surprisingly simple. Yes. Building a winning tradition actually can be expressed as building a tradition of wins or, even better, as establishing a pattern or habit of achieving small successes. In other words, a winning tradition consists of experiencing success repeatedly. A great coach intent on building a winning tradition understands this notion and actually designs practice and game plans on this idea.

Newspaper articles and sports news sound bites contain countless quotes from coaches who use the tired old cliché, "The role of a coach is to put his team in a position to be successful." Usually, this statement refers to a specific scenario, perhaps the final two minutes or the bottom of the ninth inning of a close game. A kernel of truth lies buried in that cliché or it wouldn't be a cliché. However, a great coach knows that if he waits until the final two minutes of a close game to put his team in a position to be successful, it may be too late. A great coach knows that putting a team in a position to be successful must be something that happens early and often, beginning with day one.

In order for the team to experience success early, to get early wins, a great coach designs meaningful work with success in mind for the team and for individual athletes. A great coach does not begin the first practice of the year with impossible tasks, timed drills with marks that are impossible to beat, or challenges that are insurmountable. Instead, a great coach begins with meaningful work that can be executed successfully: timed sprints with reasonable times, free-throw totals or percentages that are reachable, serving accuracy that can be attained. As players' skills improve, goals and marks can become more challenging. When a coach begins a season or even a practice with impossible goals, unrealistic expectations, and work that cannot be mastered, he robs the team of the chance to experience success. A team needs to know it can achieve success and the responsibility falls on the coach to create scenarios in which the team can experience success. The individual athletes must do the hard work, of course, but the work must be meaningful and only the coach can determine that and design the work accordingly.

The value of both individual and team wins cannot be overstated. In fact, a great coach expends tremendous energy watching at every practice and during every game in search of wins. When a quarterback completes three passes in a row for the first time, a great coach applauds the win. When a player sinks five putts in a row, a great coach acknowledges the win. When a basketball team completes a passing drill with no dropped balls, a great coach celebrates the win. Only after small, repeatable wins have been achieved can a great coach expect to raise the bar without leaving the team behind.

Men's water polo coach Terry Schroeder knows a thing or two about building a winning tradition by getting early wins. Currently the men's water polo coach at Pepperdine University, where he coached his team to an NCAA national championship, Schroeder led an underdog US water polo team to an unlikely silver medal in the 2008 Olympics. A four-time Olympian with two silver medals of his own as an athlete, Schroeder drew on his experience as a player to guide his team to success. Says Schroeder of planning for wins and early successes on his Olympic journey as a coach, "in 2007 we used the mantra 'get back to the podium.' USA Water Polo had not won a medal ('back to the podium') in 20 years. So for us to talk about winning a gold medal was over the team's head. Getting back to the podium became a realistic, reachable goal." To do something with your own team, Schroeder recommends, "Celebrate the small successes along the way. Focus on the positive changes that are happening with your team." On the road "back to the podium," the US team practiced repeatedly against a much better Serbian team. The team notched no Wins against the Serbians, but they racked up the wins. From the outside looking in, the matches against Serbia may not have seemed successful, but the small successes added up and led to greater success down the road. Schroeder adds, "Changing a culture does not happen overnight – it is a slow process and the team needs to believe that they can 'win.' It is important to stay positive during the difficult times. Talk and live as if it is going to happen. The leader needs to believe more than anyone else."

Like Schroeder with his collegiate and Olympic athletes, great teachers of all subjects and all ages can find success with the concept of getting early wins. This concept holds true for world-class athletes, high school students, middle school students, and even for the youngest of students. Imagine, for example, a kindergarten class standing in tears just minutes into the first day of school after being given the following instructions: "Please enter the classroom quietly in a single file line, find the hook on the wall below your name, hang your backpack on the appropriate hook, arrange yourselves in desks alphabetically from left to right and front to back, write two paragraphs about your summer vacation, then staple your essay to the bulletin board. Anyone not following instructions will stay in during recess to write lines." Perhaps at the end of the year, this kindergarten class could accomplish a similar list of tasks, but certainly not on the first day of school. A great kindergarten teacher finds a way to give her students simple tasks and, once the class has accomplished the tasks, celebrates the wins. The kindergarteners, rather than standing and crying in confusion, begin to believe, "We can do this." As Schroeder says, the process takes time and won't happen overnight, but it will happen. The same scenario can be applied to students of any age and any subject at any school.

As in the world of athletics, opportunities for early wins in the classroom do not happen accidentally. A great teacher plans strategically for students to experience success early and often beginning on day one. A great teacher designs meaningful work with student success in mind. Problems, assignments, or other work designed to confound students and trip them up would never be used by a great teacher looking for early wins. If a middle school math teacher early in the school year assigns problems far exceeding the students' skill level the students will develop a fear of math and a belief that they can't achieve success. A great math teacher, on the other hand, builds confidence in students by providing meaningful work designed to promote confidence and success. More challenging work, when appropriate, can promote grit, resilience, determination, and mastery of skills, but only once the great teacher has prepared the students to be successful. Even in rigorous, high-stakes courses like AP Statistics or AP Physics, a great teacher begins the year with opportunities for students to be successful then builds on those successes.

Walk into a school and ask which teachers on campus have built a winning tradition. The names of those teachers won't be a secret and it won't take long to figure out who they are. Those great teachers, like Terry Schroeder and other great coaches, all have a common denominator: they strategically and intentionally provided opportunities for students to achieve small successes, or get early wins.

3

Creating a Culture of Success

> **❝** Changing a culture does not happen overnight – it is a slow process and the team needs to believe that they can 'win.' **❞**
>
> (*Terry Schroeder*, coach of Pepperdine University men's water polo team, NCAA national champion, and Olympic medalist as athlete and coach)

When it comes to creating a culture of success, perhaps no one in college sports knows more about the subject than *Anson Dorrance*, college soccer's all-time winningest coach. As the head coach of women's soccer at the University of North Carolina, Dorrance has compiled staggering numbers during his tenure. Dorrance has won more than 92 percent of his games at UNC, and in the 30-plus years the NCAA has crowned a women's soccer national champion, UNC has claimed the title a record 22 times under his leadership. In case those numbers aren't impressive enough, more than 50 of this Hall of Famer's former players have gone on to earn caps on the US women's national team. Speaking of the US women's national team, in his spare time in 1991, Dorrance piloted the team to its first ever World Cup title.

No formula exists for creating such an impressive tradition of winning. However, Dorrance and his staff have been very strategic with a number of things over the years, not the least of which is creating a culture that breeds success on and off the pitch. Over time, Dorrance has created and fostered a culture of hard work, a culture in which player growth is encouraged – if not expected – and a culture in which players are expected to commit to a community or cause greater than themselves. The culture did not appear overnight, though. As Dorrance says of building a culture centered on life lessons, "Honestly, for years I've been one of these people that have devoured business books, and they always talk about an effective corporate culture. I never really figured out back when I was younger what was going to work in creating a culture here to help the kids grow personally. What we've done recently, which I think has made a big difference, is rather than review a mundane value like 'we work hard,' we have players memorize motivational quotes. By memorizing them it actually becomes a part of their fabric . . . We believe in a sort of principle-centered living. I think the way you teach people principles is by giving them something that will motivate them to be better in certain areas."

Part of the UNC approach to building a culture and growing players personally centers on being part of something larger than one's self and being part of a team that "doesn't whine about everything." To address this specifically, Dorrance has his players memorize *The Splendid Torch*, by George Bernard Shaw, which states in part:

> This is the true joy in life, the being used for a purpose recognized by yourself as a mighty one; the being a force of nature instead of a feverish, selfish little clod of ailments and grievances complaining that the world will not devote itself to making you happy.

> I am of the opinion that my life belongs to the whole community, and as long as I live it is my privilege to do for it whatever I can.

Dorrance got the idea from reading about a woman who, after reading and memorizing volumes of Russian poetry for a Ph.D. program, claimed the memorization changed the way she thought. Dorrance says: "it changed her cerebral fabric. It changed what she would discuss when she would speak with her colleagues about what she was studying. It completely changed her outlook. I like the part where it became a part of her cerebral fabric, because what we're trying to do by memorizing our core values is the same thing. We don't want them to be able just to recite platitudes, we want this to change behavior. And what we've discovered is that memorizing 12 different core values with a motivational quote actually impacted the behavior of our kids."

Dorrance says the emphasis on values and motivational quotes has created a sense of positive peer pressure on his team. His players actually push one another and expect each other to live by the principles and values they learn under his leadership. "A combination of the peer pressure from the players on the team, and the fact that they have memorized every motivational quote . . ., I think has helped transform our culture. There's no mystery as to what's embraced or accepted in our program – they've memorized it. I think this has made a huge difference for us."

Building a culture of success does not happen by accident. Just as Dorrance has done at the UNC, a great teacher should take very strategic steps toward building a culture of success in her classroom. What a teacher holds dear and demonstrates to be valuable sets the tone for the classroom culture. However, just as Dorrance did at UNC, a great teacher must find a way to intentionally weave the values into the "cerebral fabric" of her students. While most teachers probably will not require students to memorize 12 core values and accompanying motivational quotes, she certainly can make such motivational quotes visible to the students daily. To build a culture of success in the classroom, a great teacher should choose quotes or other motivational material that sends an empowering message and a message that hard work yields success. She can display such information on bulletin boards or whiteboards, post them to her website, use them as writing prompts, send them into cyberspace with Twitter, use them for bell-ringer activities, and more. As Dorrance likely would agree, students of any age can be impacted by seeing and hearing motivational messages with a common theme every day.

A great teacher can work toward the creation of a culture of success using more subtle techniques, too. When she publicly applauds and recognizes those things she values – like hard work, perseverance, determination, and a positive attitude – a great teacher sends a message about the kind of culture that defines her classroom. Students, like sponges, will soak up those messages. Likewise, when a great teacher publicly discourages those things she does not want as part of the classroom identity – excuses, poor effort, or negativity – students will pick up on that cultural message. As Dorrance says of his program, there should be "no mystery as to what's embraced or accepted" in the classroom. With diligence and consistency, a great teacher can establish a culture of success. Before long, like Dorrance's players, a great teacher's students will buy in to the culture and, through positive peer pressure, actually hold one another accountable. Anson Dorrance would be the first to say that memorizing quotes and committing to team values has not directly resulted in 22 national championships. Dorrance would be quick to point out, however, that impacting his players in such a big way certainly has made a difference.

4

Include Everyone

> **❝**Communities that include everyone
> become stronger and everyone wins.**❞**
>
> (Jane Imbody)

In 1976, a young freshman and junior varsity basketball coach named *Jeff Holman* took over the varsity girls tennis team at Haddonfield Memorial High School in New Jersey. Like so many young, inexperienced coaches, this young and ambitious tennis coach learned perhaps more lessons in those early years of coaching and teaching than did his players. One lesson in particular, though, would shape this young coach's approach to working with students and building a program. This one lesson would go on to shape and even define his career.

In one of his first years as varsity tennis coach at Haddonfield Memorial, Holman cut the number of varsity players to 16 so he would have a more manageable number of girls to work with during practices. Much to Holman's surprise, the number 17 girl, a freshman who didn't make the team, wouldn't go away. She often returned to the tennis courts after the varsity practices and asked Holman to work with her. The following year, the same girl returned for tryouts and made the team. She then went on to become one of the best players in school history (at a standout tennis school) and even led Haddonfield to win its first Tournament of Champions. Following an outstanding high school career, the former number-17-who-got-cut-as-a-freshman became a great collegiate player.

This experience convicted Holman and he changed his approach forever. After this experience, Holman decided to forgo cuts on his team so he could include more players. By not cutting, Holman made everyone part of the team and allowed everyone to contribute to the program. Additionally, by including everyone who wanted to participate, Holman allowed more and more players to enjoy the fruits of the program's success. And the program, under Holman's direction, has had plenty of success. In 2013, Holman notched his 1,000th win for Haddonfield in high school girls tennis, more than any other high school girls tennis coach in history. As if that feat isn't impressive enough, there's an extra wrinkle to this story. Holman took over the Haddonfield Memorial boys tennis program shortly after stepping to the helm of the girls program. In 2013, Holman led Haddonfield's boys team to its 1,000th victory, too, and solidified his spot among the top three all-time winningest high school boys tennis coaches. To be clear, the countless number of tennis players Holman has coached at Haddonfield Memorial in his 35-plus years have amassed more than 2,000 wins.

When asked about how he's been able to build and maintain such a winning tradition over the years, Holman offered some sound advice. Holman said, "I rely heavily on enthusiasm and positive reinforcement to motivate my players. I want everybody in my program – not just the varsity starters – to feel respected and appreciated, so I provide constant encouragement and focus on what players are doing right. I also feel that the team should see by my actions that I am completely dedicated to the program and expect more of myself than I do anyone else." Holman's words of wisdom should be words to live by in the classroom, too.

Like Holman, a good teacher relies on enthusiasm and positive reinforcement to motivate students. Because enthusiasm tends to be contagious, an enthusiastic teacher communicates to students a positive message about the subject being taught. An enthusiastic teacher sends the message, "I'm excited about this and you should be, too. Let me explain why . . ." An enthusiastic teacher engages students and captures their attention. Students don't want to be around people who aren't enthusiastic and they don't seek relationships with people who aren't enthusiastic. A teacher who exudes enthusiasm, though, lays the foundation for solid student relationships and attracts students like a magnet. Every school has a handful of teachers to whom the students gravitate and desire to be around. A sure bet is that those teachers have enthusiasm to spare. Positive reinforcement, like enthusiasm, engages students and communicates a positive message. A teacher who always points out flaws, errors, and shortcomings rarely motivates students to do their best and perform at a high level. A good teacher, though, knows that positive reinforcement for things like hard work and improvement motivate students better than anything else.

It can be easy for a teacher to devote a disproportionate amount of time in a classroom to the academic stars. The students who grasp concepts easily, who overachieve, who always ask questions, and who always answer questions correctly often make teaching seem pretty easy and they unwittingly can draw a teacher's attention away from the quieter, less academically talented students. Holman's desire for everyone in his program to feel respected and appreciated, not just the varsity starters, serves as a great reminder for teachers. An effective teacher goes out of her way to engage everyone in the classroom, not just the ones who are the varsity equivalent. An effective teacher, especially one who desires to build a tradition of success in her classroom, finds ways to include every student in class discussions, problem solving at the board, and other ways that make them feel part of the group in a positive way. One of the best ways a teacher does this is by providing encouragement and focusing on what students do right. What student doesn't want to be acknowledged and encouraged for something done right, especially in front of peers? Holman gets this and so does the effective teacher.

Holman's final piece of useful advice for teachers could be deduced even if he hadn't articulated the advice. Having observed Holman's actions for decades now, his former and current teams and players have no doubt about Holman's complete dedication to his program. A good teacher's actions send the same message. When students believe that a science teacher eats, sleeps, and breathes science, they sense their teacher's dedication. When students see their assignments and projects graded and returned quickly, they see evidence of dedication. When a teacher works hard in the classroom all week then attends the game or the concert on Friday night, students see firsthand his or her dedication. Like Holman, a good teacher knows that students will dedicate themselves to that to which their teacher or coach demonstrates dedication. Whether on the tennis court or in the classroom, qualities like inclusiveness, enthusiasm, encouragement, and dedication go a long way toward building and sustaining a tradition of success. Just ask Jeff Holman.

5

Magic Stickers

> **"**The way positive reinforcement is carried out is more important than the amount.**"**
>
> (B.F. Skinner)

Football historians and students of the game remember the decade of the 1960s as one of the roughest, toughest decades of football in history. In terms of safety and protection, helmets and pads in the 1960s paled in comparison to today's high-tech, ultra-protective equipment. Rules of the game in the 1960s allowed for more violent hits, fewer restrictions on contact between players, and more bone-crushing play overall than current football rules allow. It should be no surprise, then, that some of the meanest football players ever, like Dick Butkus, and notoriously tough coaches, like Woody Hayes and Bear Bryant, made their mark on football during the 1960s.

Another interesting piece of football history emerged during the 1960s, too. Although credited to a number of different football coaches, including the aforementioned Woody Hayes of Ohio State University, the use of the helmet sticker arrived on the football scene early in the decade and spread like wildfire. College football coaches awarded the small stickers, which usually portrayed the school mascot or some other image symbolic of the player's college or university, for individual or team accomplishments. Over the next several decades, and continuing even today, outstanding college football players often sported helmets covered with buckeye leaf stickers, or paw-print stickers or tomahawk stickers, depending on their school, of course. The coaches used these stickers to recognize players and their accomplishments not only in front of their peers but also in front of stadiums full of fans. Believe it or not, football players for decades have loved to work hard for those stickers.

Before academicians everywhere get worked up over the body of work in the fields of educational and behavioral psychology arguing that extrinsic rewards have led to the demise of American education, let's be reasonable about these helmet stickers. A great coach never would misunderstand the true nature and intent of these stickers. A great coach would use these simple stickers as rewards for successes, for wins, but never as a substitute for intrinsic motivation, grit, or determination. No college football player works harder in practice, runs faster on the field, and dives for extra yardage simply to earn a new sticker for his helmet, nor would a great coach expect him to do so. A great coach sees a helmet sticker for what it is: a simple but meaningful way to applaud a win, or perhaps even a Win.

Whether these rough and tumble football coaches borrowed the idea of using stickers for rewards from elementary teachers, we may never know. Perhaps one of these tough guys received a sticker in first grade for acing a spelling test or staying in his seat until recess. This we do know, though: elementary teachers have used the proverbial "gold star" for who knows how long to reward good behavior and to recognize students for a job well done. Over time, the gold star morphed into scratch-and-sniff stickers and puffy stickers and holo-gram stickers. At the end of the day, though, the concepts of positive reinforcement for desired behavior and acknowledging and applaud-ing wins remain the same.

While younger children respond better to rewards like gold star stickers or stamps, kids of all ages enjoy recognition for achievements and successes, for wins. Even middle and high school kids will bend over backwards to earn a seemingly insignificant prize for a job well done. There are plenty of high school students who would be blown away if a teacher stuck gold stars on their essays and hung the essays on the bulletin board for their classmates to see. Imagine, for example, a student who writes an essay but turns it in unsure of whether the essay has met the teacher's expectations. Now imagine the same student and her reaction at seeing the essay on display for all to see and branded permanently with a "Great job!" stamp or sticker. A great teacher does this often, or at least variations of this, regardless of the ages of her students. A great teacher also knows that simple rewards like public praise or gold star stickers could never replace intrinsic motivation and intangible values like grit and determination in a classroom where she is building a winning tradition. Rather, the public praise and gold star stickers highlight and acknowledge wins. A token economy would not be the goal of a great teacher using occasional positive reinforcement, but rather an environment in which success is promoted, appreciated, and applauded. Because success breeds success, students, like college football players, need acknowledgment from time to time of their successes, maybe even with stickers.

Section VI

Teach Life Lessons

1

The Extra Work Makes the Difference

"The lessons I want to teach are simple as can be, but they must not be that easy, because not many people **"** in this world seem to be able to follow them anymore.

(Bo Schembechler, from *Bo's Lasting Lessons: The Legendary Coach Teaches the Timeless Fundamentals of Leadership* by Bo Schembechler and John U. Bacon)

As the global economy becomes more competitive in virtually every way, simply being good enough, smart enough, or skilled enough will not provide anyone a competitive edge in the twenty-first century. To be competitive in the twenty-first century, competency, intelligence, and skill must be combined with a powerful work ethic. The sports world provides numerous opportunities for teaching such life lessons. To be competitive in the twenty-first-century world of competitive sports, successful players and teams cannot practice merely the number of minutes allotted to them by their respective governing bodies for official practice time. The best coaches teach their teams and players to work before or after practice and perhaps even year-round to be the best. Teams and players who do not put in extra time hardly can hope to compete.

To be competitive and successful, teams and players must put in a significant amount of meaningful work in addition to the official practice time. Physically, players must work out and push their bodies beyond what coaches can provide during practice time. To maintain a competitive edge, players must keep their bodies in peak physical condition not only in season but also during the offseason. Players must practice skills repeatedly both in season and in the offseason to keep their skills sharp. Practice minutes alone do not provide adequate time for all the work teams and players need to be successful. However, the better prepared teams and players are both physically and mentally going into practice, the more productive coaches can be with them during practice time. No amount of offseason or outside-of-practice work can replace the power of a great coach, but teams and players who put in outside work can empower the coach to be more effective.

One football coach in particular in Baton Rouge, Louisiana, understands this concept as well as any coach in the game today. *Kenny Guillot* took over a weak football program with a losing record at Parkview Baptist School, yet captured a state title in just his third year at the helm. Since then, Guillot has led his team to three more state championships and has amassed more than 160 wins with his Parkview football teams. Playing teams often more physically gifted or athletic than his, Guillot knows how to equalize things and level the playing field. "We say we win championships between January and August [the offseason] because we feel we have an offseason training program that's second to none," says Guillot. In other words, the work Parkview's players put in during the offseason actually gives them an edge or advantage during the season. Though Guillot's players cannot hold official practices during the offseason, per regulations of the state athletic governing body, they train as hard during the offseason as they do during the official football season. Why do they work so hard when they don't have to? Guillot explains, "Great players, great teams and great organizations have one common denominator: a work ethic that is second to none. We stress to our kids the importance of working hard on everything we do in season and during the offseason. We tell them our work ethic is our great equalizer. Additionally, our players want to be as good as or better than the ones before them, in a positive way."

Guillot's lesson about extra work transfers to the classroom easily. One of the key elements of success – whether in the global economy, the job application process, college applications and admissions, the race for valedictorian, mastering a second language, or even learning to read – lies in a student's willingness to put in work outside of instructional time in the classroom. The learning process may begin with great teaching in the classroom, but a student must practice outside of class. A student learning to read will not excel if the only time he reads is during class. A student learning a second language will not master the language if his only practice with the language occurs five times per week during second period. Math skills, writing skills, reading skills, spelling, and more must be practiced outside the classroom.

A good teacher, like a good coach, emphasizes to her students the importance of work and practice outside the classroom. More often than not, and barring some extenuating circumstance out of a student's control, a direct correlation exists between a student's work ethic and his ability to master concepts and excel in the classroom, just as with an athlete and his mastery of certain skills. Like athletes in the sports world, few students have the natural ability to coast through school with little or no effort and excel academically. Most students must put forth effort to experience academic success. Those students who work hard usually see the fruits of their labor and experience success in proportion to their work ethic. Furthermore, as Guillot says is the case with his teams, hard work may be an equalizer for many students. While some students acquire skills more easily than others, hard work can level the playing field. The same applies when students encounter a difficult course or concept in school: when innate ability or intelligence turns out to be not quite enough for mastery, a little hard work goes a long way.

While some students may be driven and intrinsically motivated, many students need a good teacher to inspire, to motivate, and to push. The importance of a strong work ethic cannot be overstated, especially when the world shrinks and flattens at such a high rate of speed. In an often unpredictable world, one thing can be predicted with certainty. Literally millions of students worldwide have plotted for themselves a course for success in the global economy and their plans rely heavily on work ethic. Coach Guillot reminds his players often that they may get beaten by better teams but they will never even face a team that works harder than Parkview. Imagine the impact a good teacher could make by emphasizing this important life lesson in the classroom regularly. After all, the life lessons about work ethic learned both in the classroom and on the athletic field may have as much impact on students' lives as science, math, or other academic lessons.

2

The Honest Truth About Cheating

> **❝**It's important that athletes can compete on a level
> playing field. And youngsters coming into the sport
> can know that if they are working hard and training
> hard, they'll see a true reflection of where they
> stand and what they can achieve worldwide
> and not be swayed by people who are cheating. **❞**
>
> (Paula Radcliffe, accomplished marathon runner and
> current women's marathon world record holder)

Let's face it. Life is full of cheaters and cheating, and it's becoming
tougher every year to fight dishonesty and dissuade students from
cheating. The annals of sports contain too many cheating incidents
to chronicle here. The shortlist of some of the more memorable cheaters, though, includes cyclist Lance Armstrong, Olympic skater Tonya
Harding, Olympic sprinter Ben Johnson, the 2008 Chinese Olympic
gymnastics officials, marathon runner Rosie Ruiz, Soviet Olympic
fencer Boris Onischenko, soccer phenom Diego Maradona, and most
recently Major League Baseball player Ryan Braun. These incidents
would be bad enough, but the sports world reflects the real world.
Unfortunately, there are plenty of memorable, high-profile cases of
cheating outside the sports world. History will always remember

Enron's Ken Lay and Jeffrey Skilling, Ponzi scheme masterminds Barry Minkow and Bernie Madoff, and "Twenty-One" game show whiz Charles Van Doren, as cheaters. To make matters even worse for the players and students under the tutelage of quality coaches and teachers, recent years have given us examples of teachers and coaches cheating, too. Scores of teachers and administrators have been found guilty of altering test scores across the United States, and during the 2013 season football coaching staff at a Louisiana high school gained unauthorized access to a rival school's Hudl account and spent nearly 12 hours studying their game film and game plan. In the face of such disheartening news, what are coaches and teachers to do to combat cheating and to encourage kids to make good choices?

Duke men's basketball coach Mike Krzyzewski, or "Coach K," approaches cheating in a powerful way. In his book *Leading with the Heart: Coach K's Successful Strategies for Basketball, Business, and Life*, Coach K explains his approach to confronting his players with the issue of academic integrity. He asks his players during a team meeting about the worst thing that can happen to them academically. Invariably, they respond that getting an F would be the worst. Coach K responds with, "No, that's not the worst thing . . . You can get an F even if you try like crazy. The worst thing you can do is cheat." He then goes on to address specific ways players might cheat academically and explains that those all are "unacceptable" at Duke. Coach K then addresses issues like time management, how to avoid being in a compromising position, and asking for help.

Coach K's approach carries weight with his players for a number of reasons. First, he makes it clear that failure, receiving an F, may happen regardless of effort. He also implies that failure, an F, in the face of effort is acceptable while cheating absolutely is unacceptable. Second, he clarifies his values and the values of his institution by declaring cheating as "unacceptable" in the Duke basketball program. Third, he says clearly that cheating is the worst thing that can happen academically, without exception. Duke's players respect and value Coach K as a coach, a teacher, a leader, and as a person. What Coach K says impacts his players. They listen and take his words to heart. Because he understands this, Coach K leverages his influence to make a positive impact on his players' lives.

Teachers can, and should, steal this page from Coach K's playbook. Teachers can have a powerful impact on the lives of their students. A good teacher who knows how much difference he can make in the lives of his students should leverage that influence and address cheating head on. Using Coach K's approach, a good teacher can honestly and genuinely communicate to his students, regardless of their ages, that missing the mark academically is not the worst thing that the students can do, but rather that cheating is the worst.

In order for Coach K's approach to be successful, two things must happen. First, the teacher must have a relationship with the students, and specifically a relationship built on mutual trust and respect. Coach K's words hold sway over his players because of just such a relationship that he builds with his players year in and year out. Without such a relationship, the potentially powerful message about academic integrity holds little value. Second, the teacher must establish an environment in which students have the freedom to fail. Ideally, the teacher establishes what Augie Garrido, legendary baseball coach from the University of Texas, calls the "fearless field." The fearless field – whether it be an actual baseball field, a classroom, etc. – is a place where people do not fear failure and risk taking. In a classroom, it will be entirely up to the teacher to create such an environment. So often, students who cheat do so because of the fear of failure. For those students, a fearless field may liberate them from such crippling choices as cheating. Granted, creating a fearless field may help curb cheating only in that classroom initially, but cheating – in sports, in school, or in the real world – is a heart issue. Heart issues must be addressed through influence, not rules, and it just may be the influence of a good coach or teacher that extends beyond the court or the classroom walls into players' and students' lives.

3

Responding Appropriately to Adversity

> **❝**I have experienced a great deal of success *and* failure, and there are lessons in both.**❞**
>
> (*Terry Schroeder*, coach of Pepperdine University men's water polo team, NCAA national champion, and Olympic medalist as athlete and coach)

The athletic arena provides coaches myriad opportunities to work with young people on putting adversity in the proper perspective and responding appropriately to adversity. These opportunities avail themselves in every sport, but perhaps no sport provides such opportunities more often than baseball. Baseball coaches and players measure success and failure a little differently than coaches and players in most other sports. For example, an exceptional hitter gets a hit one out of every three trips to the plate. An exceptional hitter fails twice as often as he succeeds. Those numbers leave average hitters successful only one out of every four trips to the plate! Here's another surprising example of how baseball coaches and players measure success. For professional baseball teams who play 162 games every season, excellent clubs win 100–110 of the 162 games. An excellent team still loses almost 40 percent of the games in a season! With success so often represented by such surprising statistics, baseball coaches must be able to keep things in perspective and keep players focused on the big picture, thus imparting valuable life lessons.

Few baseball coaches have demonstrated how to teach such life lessons as well as the late John Scolinos. Scolinos, who coached at Pepperdine, at Cal Poly Pomona, and for the US Olympic baseball team, won three national championships and three Coach of the Year awards. He retired in 1991 with nearly 1,200 victories. During his successful tenures, Scolinos encountered plenty of losses and coached players through countless setbacks like strikeouts at the plate, errors in the field, walked batters, hitting slumps, losing streaks, and more. However, Scolinos approached these setbacks as opportunities to teach his young men how to handle adversity. He turned baseball's numerous opportunities for failure and adversity into teachable moments.

Scolinos used strikeouts and fielding errors to teach his players to handle failure. By examining the fear of making errors or choking at the plate, he taught his players to confront and manage their fear. When his players faced the ups and downs of hitters' batting slumps, pitchers' rising ERAs (earned run averages), teams' losing streaks, and players' multiple fielding errors, Scolinos taught his players about handling setbacks. Scolinos even capitalized on potentially embarrassing situations like striking out to end a game and getting picked off at first base to teach the appropriate ways to handle embarrassment. In short, Scolinos taught his players to keep things in perspective, to remember the big picture, and never to allow a setback to sink a player emotionally. Furthermore, such setbacks in baseball provide opportunities to improve. Scolinos knew that teaching his players how to handle adversity on the field would equip them to handle adversity better long after they had played their last baseball games.

Classroom teachers enjoy similar opportunities daily to equip and train students to handle adversity. Though teachers don't encounter actual strikeouts and fielding errors, losing streaks and hit batters, teachers encounter students struggling and stumbling often. For a teacher with the right outlook, these hiccups present opportunities to teach life lessons just as Scolinos did with his players.

How can a teacher impart these lessons? A teacher can remind students often that mistakes are part of learning. A teacher can respond to each student's stumble and struggle with encouragement rather than chastisement, with a focus on learning and improving rather than punishment. A teacher can communicate the big picture to students rather than focusing on the minutiae of mistakes and errors. When a batting average of .333 earns a baseball slugger kudos, surely an 80 percent on a test isn't the end of the world. When a student stumbles and performs poorly on a quiz, surely the semester grade hasn't been wrecked. When a student struggles with radicals or verb conjugation or developing a thesis, surely, in the grand scheme of the course, such a hiccup must be just one more opportunity to improve and to grow. Here lie the opportunities for teachers to do as Scolinos did so many times and equip their students not to overreact or to allow frustration to ruin their outlook. Here lie the opportunities for teachers to teach students how to handle adversity.

4

Staying Focused on the Process

66 We focus on the process. We all want to win hockey games or reach our goals, but how do we do that? For us, we have done it by focusing on a certain number of things in games. We can't focus on winning, we have to focus on how . . . the process. **99**

(*Brad Frost*, head coach of two-time NCAA national champion University of Minnesota women's ice hockey team)

The current state of sports worldwide makes teaching and learning life lessons difficult for coaches, especially for those in high-stakes, high-pressure positions. When the world values scoring, winning, and results to the extent it does today, finding value in anything other than results can be difficult for athletes, especially young ones. The world judges and evaluates coaches, players, and teams based on wins, margins of victory, titles, and other performance-based criteria. Coaches, players, and teams rise to glory or fall from grace based on quantified results. Young athletes know this and feel the pressure to win perhaps now more than ever. The opportunities for teaching life lessons abound, but the challenge of driving those life lessons home with athletes often increases as the stage grows larger and the pressure intensifies. *Sean Fleming*, head coach of Canada Soccer's U-17 (under 17 years of age) men's national team, understands this as well as anyone.

In 2013, Fleming led his young men through a series of qualifying matches and earned a second consecutive trip to the FIFA U-17 World Cup. For a nation like Canada, whose men's national team has struggled on the world stage in recent years, the soccer hopes of the nation rest squarely on the shoulders of the U-17 team. As the Canadian Soccer Association website says, "The FIFA U-17 World Cup is an important step in player development en route to Canada's national 'A' squad." After all, in only a few years, the U-17 players are the young men who will represent their nation in the quest for the FIFA World Cup, international football's (soccer's) greatest achievement.

A former teacher who spent 13 years in the classroom before moving to soccer full-time, Fleming knows the pressure bearing down on his young men. He also knows that part of developing and molding his players involves teaching them life lessons and equipping them to handle real-life situations outside of soccer. On the national and international stages, every match becomes a high-stakes, high-pressure situation. To keep his players zeroed in on what's important, Fleming says, "I try to focus not on the results but on the process. I do this through emphasis on growth and repetition. I really try to emphasize the skill development and player growth." Even when the world values performance above all else, Fleming redirects his players' attention and emphasizes mastery, or skill development and player growth, rather than performance. Undoubtedly, Fleming wants to win and perform as much as anyone else in the business. However, Fleming knows the wins will come as long as his players continue to grow and develop, so his emphasis must be first and foremost on mastery, not on performance.

The most challenging time to teach life lessons to young athletes in such a high-pressure situation often comes after a loss. Losing is never fun, but losing an international match on a world stage is enough to rattle any young person. When this situation arises, Fleming works to refocus his players. "After a loss, I always return to the process, to points of emphasis." Emphasis on growth, development, and mastery of skills shifts the players' attention away solely from the performance.

Furthermore, Fleming says, "I also try to learn from those situations myself, make sure I don't overreact." He knows his players watch him and follow his lead. It wouldn't take long for Fleming's players to pick up on his disingenuousness if he overreacted to a loss then preached to the team about returning their focus to the process and to points of emphasis.

Coaches, players, and teams share a common burden with teachers, students, and schools of the twenty-first century. Like their athletic counterparts, teachers, students, and schools find themselves more than ever evaluated based on scores and quantified results. Lawmakers and administrators tie teacher salaries and contracts to scores. Lawmakers and administrators allocate financial resources to districts and buildings based on scores. Schools, teachers, and colleges evaluate students based on scores. With every new test, exam, and set of scores, the stakes become higher and higher for teachers, students, and schools. In such a high-stakes environment, students easily can glean the wrong message, the message that results matter more than the process, and that performance matters more than mastery.

Amidst the rising pressure for improved test scores, Fleming's advice will resonate with a good teacher. A good teacher knows test results and scores eventually will improve as long as students continue to grow and develop. Therefore, a good teacher emphasizes the process more than the results. Even in a course that culminates with a high-stakes exam, as with an Advanced Placement course, placing the emphasis on the results alone sends the message that the results are more important than the learning process. If students constantly hear the message that results are more important than the process, they head into life valuing grades and scores more than learning and improvement. When things get tough for Fleming and his team, he shifts the focus back to the process and the points of emphasis he and his staff have been teaching. An effective teacher does the same thing in the classroom.

Fleming's plan for focusing on the process, student growth, and skill development works equally well on a smaller scale such as the day-to-day classroom routine. An English or language arts teacher, for example, must coach her students on the process of writing. If she primarily emphasizes turning in a great research paper or essay at the expense of emphasizing the writing process, the students receive the message that the final product has more value than the writing process. If this were true, students would take research papers and essays into the world with them. Instead, students take skills with them. A good teacher knows she must emphasize the importance of mastering language and writing skills more so than performing well on any given writing assignment. An emphasis on mastery more than performance may be counter-cultural in today's test-driven, results-driven world, but a good teacher, like former teacher Sean Fleming, understands that educators must constantly return to the process and points of emphasis. Furthermore, a good teacher who teaches students to focus on the process sends those students into the world empowered to consider their own growth and development, and better equipped to handle disappointment. What a great life lesson.

5

Reduce Stress with the Process

" Getting them to enjoy the process . . . I have to get
my guys to enjoy the process of going through the
drills, the process of 'I got a chance to work on my
single-leg today, I'm healthy, I have the opportunity to
wrestle and do something I'm gifted at, I'm going to
enjoy the battle today. At the end of practice when I'm
totally drenched in sweat, and every muscle in my
body is killing me, I love it. I'm a warrior and I got to
do something I love to do.' The more that they love the
process, the more meaningful those drills in practice are.
The more they love the process, they put less pressure
on themselves when it comes to the anxiety "
of accomplishing their objectives down the road.

(*Brandon Slay*, USA Wrestling coach and
2000 Olympic gold medalist in wrestling)

Without a doubt, athletes at all levels face more stress than ever.
Athletes on the international stage competing for national pride,
professional and collegiate athletes whose performances translate to
millions of dollars, collegiate athletes who aspire to play professionally,
high school athletes who want a chance at scholarship opportunities,

youth sports athletes who want to please their coaches, parents, and peers – all these athletes wrestle with stress. Believe it or not, though, stress can be very beneficial for athletes . . . up to the point that it isn't.

Great coaches know that the appropriate amount of stress actually benefits athletes and their performance. Research now over a century old provides the framework for what has become known as the Yerkes–Dodson Law. According to the Yerkes–Dodson Law, there exists a direct correlation between performance and arousal, i.e. stress, nerves, or anxiety. In other words, increased arousal, stress, nerves, or anxiety increases performance up to the point the arousal becomes excessive.

Consider a field goal kicker trotting on to a football field to kick a long but game-winning field goal. If the kicker experiences the appropriate amount of stress, perhaps realizing the importance of the kick and the significance of his role in his team's success and enjoying the excitement of the opportunity, he becomes focused on the task at hand, his skills and concentration are sharpened, and he becomes more likely to deliver an accurate kick that splits the uprights and seals the win for his team. On the other hand, if the kicker allows himself to become too worked up, stressed, and – to use the Yerkes–Dodson terminology – too aroused, the excessive stress likely will cause his performance to decrease. In other words, the kicker may choke. This is why opposing coaches often call "Timeout" just before a kicker attempts such a kick; opposing coaches hope the kicker overthinks the situation during the timeout and falls victim to the downside of the Yerkes–Dodson Law.

Coaches rarely have to increase the amount of stress on athletes to get them to perform at optimum levels. Rather, coaches often have to help players manage their stress and help them cope with it. A great coach knows each of his players and knows at what point on a continuum lies that player's appropriate stress level for optimum performance. When a player's stress exceeds that point, the coach must intervene and reduce the stress or help the player reduce his own stress. But how? Where does this stress come from, and how can the stress be managed?

Marv Dunphy offers a pretty convincing theory on athletes' stress. As a coach who has led his Pepperdine University men's volleyball team to five NCAA national championships and Team USA men's volleyball to a 1988 Olympic gold medal, Coach Dunphy knows a thing or two about stress. Says Dunphy of stress on athletes, "Stress comes from the uncertainty of the outcome. You have to have a plan to lower anxiety, but the uncertainty of the outcome is what causes stress in sport and, probably, in life, too." According to Dunphy, a coach can help reduce the stress and lower anxiety for his players. He looks to coaching greats like UCLA men's basketball legend John Wooden and NFL legend Bill Walsh as examples. "They took it beyond this win/lose, you make this free throw you win, you miss, you choke, you lose . . . They took it beyond this win/lose . . . and as a result their teams played free, they played at a higher level. It took the stress out . . ." In other words, Wooden and Walsh focused less on the win/lose, or the uncertain outcome, and focused more on the plan and the process. As Dunphy explains, athletes' confidence must be in the process, their training and their plan, because that can be certain. The outcome – winning or losing on a large scale, making or missing a shot on a smaller scale – remains, on the other hand, entirely uncertain, and that is what causes stress. Echoing Wooden and Walsh, Dunphy emphasizes, "You have to focus on the process and not so much the results."

Like today's athletes, today's students feel more pressure and stress than ever. As with athletes on the field or in the arena, students benefit from the appropriate amount of stress. A little anxiety about a test, a speech, a performance, an interview, or a presentation can give a student an edge and help her excel. Too much stress, though, can paralyze the student and cause her performance to decrease in the same way too much stress might cause a kicker to choke before an important field goal attempt. A great teacher can borrow a page from Dunphy's playbook, though, and help students reduce excessive stress by shifting the focus from the uncertain outcome – the A, the award, the admissions acceptance – to the certainty of the process.

In the classroom, reducing stress by emphasizing the process involves first having a plan. Whether students are learning the alphabet, learning to read, learning a second language, learning quadratic equations, or learning Shakespeare, they need a plan for mastering what they are learning. A great teacher certainly will have a plan that involves meaningful work, meaningful assessment, and meaningful feedback along the way, and her students will know she has a plan. With any of these examples, though, students eventually will have to put their learning to the test and will be assessed in some way, just like a kicker and his field goal or a basketball player at the free throw line. In some cases, the assessment might be a classroom test, quiz, demonstration, or presentation, while in other cases the assessment may be a high-stakes state or College Board exam. In either scenario, students very likely will experience some amount of stress headed into the assessment.

A great teacher who wants her students to perform free and at a higher level, to borrow Dunphy's words, keeps her students focused more on the certainty of what they've learned and how they've learned it than on the uncertainty of the outcome. To put it differently, a great teacher will not let her students worry about and focus on the test results, the final grade, or the final score. Instead, a great teacher redirects her students and instills confidence in them by reminding them of the quality work and learning they've done. It is that quality work and learning that will empower the students to be successful, and that process is the one thing about which both teacher and students can be certain. After all, as Dunphy explains, the uncertainty of the outcome is the source of stress. A great teacher remains continuously sensitive to this stress and, like Wooden, Walsh, and Dunphy, takes the learning experience beyond win/lose, pass/fail, A/B, etc. By teaching and modeling to students the value of focusing on the certainty of the process rather than on the uncertainty of the outcome, a great teacher can engrain in her students one of the same powerful life lessons that Coach Marv Dunphy has engrained in his national champions and his Olympians.

6

Problem Solving Isn't Enough

> **"** If I were given one hour to save the planet,
> I would spend 59 minutes defining **"**
> the problem and one minute resolving it.
>
> (Albert Einstein)

Few of history's great innovators, inventors, and entrepreneurs achieved prominence by being only problem solvers. Rather, most of history's greatest game-changers achieved fame and fortune because they first identified a problem, a need, or a niche. Only after they identified the problem could they set out to solve the problem, meet the need, or fill the niche. History credits these game-changers for their problem-solving prowess yet seldom applauds their ability to identify problems first. The same has been true, and remains true, in the world of sports. The inventors of such things as the forward pass in football, the curveball or the bunt in baseball, zone defense or the hook shot in basketball, the overhand jump serve in volleyball, the wall in soccer, and the Fosbury Flop in track and field, to name just a few, first identified areas of their respective sports that needed improvement and then they innovated and developed solutions.

The same principle applies to some of the greatest, most successful athletes. The greatest passers in football history certainly have enjoyed problem-solving skills. Nearly every play from the line of scrimmage presents a puzzle for the quarterback to solve. One of the things that sets apart players like Joe Montana, Peyton Manning, and Drew Brees from all others, though, has been their ability to step to the line of scrimmage, glance at the opposing defense, and make a proper read and adjustment. In other words, these great quarterbacks have had the uncanny ability to quickly identify a problem on the field in the middle of a game, then make a split-second assessment followed by a problem-solving decision that allows him to successfully complete a pass. The key here is this: a quarterback can't solve a problem successfully if he can't first identify the problem, or set up the problem in his mind so that he can find a solution. Many quarterbacks could make necessary adjustments, or could problem solve successfully, if someone else identifies the problem for them and explains the ideal solution. The best, however, do it on their own. They first identify the problem, and usually very quickly, then they problem solve.

Basketball provides even more great examples of players first identifying problems then solving the problems. In basketball, the point guard acts in much the same way as a football quarterback in terms of reading the defense and making decisions about how best to attack. An adequate point guard may be able to communicate with the coach on the sideline each trip down the floor, process the input received from the coach, and then execute the appropriate play. Great point guards like Magic Johnson, John Stockton, and Jason Kidd, though, could identify problems and problem solve quickly and under pressure. If a point guard sees the opposing team in a 2–3 zone defense, for example, and decides to attack the even-front defense with an odd-man attack, he has assessed the problem and solved it. As with the quarterback, the point guard could not have solved the problem if he had not first been able to identify the problem or set up the problem in his mind.

Sports like golf and soccer offer more insight into the idea of identifying problems first before solving them. In golf, a golfer must correctly identify scores of problems during every round, literally before every single swing of the club or stroke of the putter. If a golfer can't accurately assess a problem, or set up a problem in his or her mind, the golf ball will end up anywhere except near the flagstick. Even when a golfer has a caddie to offer data like wind speed and distance to the hole, the golfer still must set up the problem in his mind before creating a solution for the problem. In soccer, coaches rely heavily on soccer players' ability to identify and solve problems during the course of the game. During soccer matches, very little coaching and game management occurs from the sidelines. Rather, preparation for matches happens almost entirely during practice and players manage the flow of matches on their own, identifying and solving problems for themselves, with little input from coaches. This model provides a good glimpse into just how great coaches train players to identify problems and then problem solve.

Great coaches want all their players, not just the quarterbacks and point guards, to develop skills in the areas of identifying problems and solving problems. In most sports, just as with real-life situations that players will encounter in the real world, things change quickly and often without warning, thus putting players in positions to constantly assess and reassess problems before attempting to solve those problems. Great coaches know that they can't always provide direct feedback to players during the course of games and matches, so the players must be equipped to identify and solve problems on their own. Players must be able to correctly set up the problem in their minds, otherwise their solutions won't solve the actual problems. Learning to identify and assess problems successfully takes time, practice, and the right kind of teaching from coaches.

Teaching players to identify problems and then solve problems requires a number of steps. First, a great coach makes sure that players have mastered the basic, fundamental concepts of the game. A quarterback can't accurately assess a situation if he doesn't fully understand the difference between man and zone coverage. If he sees zone and thinks man, he has neither identified the problem nor correctly set up the problem in his mind; therefore, any solution he devises will not solve the problem. Second, a great coach builds on the fundamentals by teaching players to analyze and assess what they observe based on the fundamental concepts they have mastered. This requires repetition, question and answer, trial and error, and plenty of meaningful work or practice. Players must be able to understand the relationships between the fundamental concepts and make connections, predict *if x then y*, and explain cause and effect relationships. Only when players can analyze situations successfully in this way can they identify problems. Nothing short of hands-on experience during which players can learn from both small successes and failures will equip players to be successful with this. Finally, a great coach trains players to synthesize a solution to the problem. But how does a coach actually teach this? There are two very important ways.

A coach can lecture his players. A coach can show video. A coach can assign reading. A coach can run his players through drills. A great coach, however, knows that nothing beats experience for developing players' abilities in terms of identifying problems and synthesizing or creating accurate solutions for those problems. Therefore, the first way a coach can teach and train players to identify and solve problems is to allow his players to learn from the game. Actual game experience provides the most meaningful learning opportunities but actual game time is limited. Therefore, a great coach uses practice time to provide game-like situations in which his players can identify problems and solve them as much as possible on their own. In practice, because the stakes aren't high, players can be encouraged by a great coach to think and play freely and creatively, exploring options and then assessing afterward the success of each option. A great coach doesn't solve all the problems for his players, nor does a great coach even set up all the problems for his players. The bottom line is that a great coach creates realistic, game-like situations for his players so they can experience the same ebb and flow, successes and failures, they would in a game so they can learn from the process.

The second way a coach can teach and train players to successfully identify problems and then solve them is by helping players ask the right questions. A great coach knows that asking not just any questions, but the right questions, can be the difference between success and failure for his players. A great coach constantly reminds his players to ask the right questions and even models this for his players. A golf coach would not be satisfied with a golfer who asks, before teeing off on a par three hole, "Can I hit the ball that far?" because that isn't the right question. A great golf coach would explain that the question the golfer just asked doesn't really shed much light on the problem. The right questions, or questions the coach would want the golfer to ask instead, might include, "Which direction is the wind blowing, and at what speed? How fast are the greens today? What's the pin location? Are there any hazards surrounding the green? What's the elevation of the green?" These questions help identify the problem or set up the problem. Players should constantly be asking questions, especially the right questions. By asking the right questions, they can begin to set up the problems in their minds and work toward successfully solving those problems.

A striking parallel exists between the athletic arena and the classroom when it comes to identifying problems and solving problems. Certainly success for today's students in the twenty-first century will require problem-solving skills. Simply put, those skills will not be enough. Only those students who possess the ability to correctly identify problems before trying to problem solve will distinguish themselves in a world whose landscape changes monthly, weekly, and sometimes daily. As in the athletic arena under the tutelage of a great coach, learning to identify problems in the classroom requires the guidance of a great teacher.

Teachers have been working for years on developing and fostering problem-solving skills in students of all ages and in all content areas. The de-emphasis on rote memorization and the emphasis on application and creativity in recent years serve as good evidence of the progress education has made in this area. Perhaps, though, not enough attention has been paid to the concept of teaching students to first identify problems before solving them. As long as teachers provide problems for students to work out or solve, students will leave classrooms missing one crucial piece of the puzzle. In an ever-changing world, students must be able to first identify and set up problems for themselves before they begin the problem-solving process. Just as athletes can't always rely on coaches to provide insight and feedback about what play to run, students can't always count on having adults around to assess situations and provide a framework for them to solve problems as they arrive. Just like the quarterback stepping to the line of scrimmage, a twenty-first-century student will need the ability to survey and assess a situation, identify a problem and set up a problem in his mind, then think analytically to synthesize and create a solution for the problem. Only a student with this ability will be the next Steve Jobs, Mark Zuckerburg, or the like. But how can this happen in the classroom?

Just as the great coach does with his players, a great teacher must begin by putting her students in a position to successfully identify and solve problems. First, a great teacher makes sure that players have mastered the basic, fundamental concepts of the game. She does this through effective communication, solid teaching, and providing meaningful work and practice for students. Second, a great teacher builds on the fundamentals by teaching players to analyze and assess what they observe based on the fundamental concepts they have mastered. This requires repetition, question and answer, trial and error, and plenty of hands-on activities that provide practical applications for what's been learned. Only once students can analyze situations successfully in this way can they identify problems. Nothing short of hands-on experience during which students can learn from both small successes and failures will equip players to be successful with this. Worksheets and questions from the textbook chapter will not work. Finally, a great teacher trains students to synthesize a solution or solutions to a problem once it has been identified. This training mirrors the training a great coach does with his players.

As with great coaching, a great teacher can make two crucial adjustments to equip her students with the ability to identify problems before solving them. First, like the great coach who provides meaningful, game-like situations during practice in which his players can hone this skill, a great teacher can design or redesign as much of her classroom experience as possible to simulate real-life situations. This can happen in any grade and in any content area. Answering multiple choice questions and solving equations does not mirror real life. Additionally, the more often teachers provide the problems for students, the more opportunities teachers miss to teach students to identify then solve problems on their own. Using word problems or story problems that provide information and data yet do not set up the actual problem or equation may be a great place to begin changing things in the classroom. Story problems can be used with any student that can read in many content areas. Well-designed story problems require students to first have a mastery of basic concepts – perhaps multiplication, for example – and then require students to set up a multiplication problem in order to solve the dilemma presented in the story. Such questions can touch on many levels of Bloom's Taxonomy and ultimately require students to demonstrate knowledge, comprehension, application, and then, for the final answer, analysis and synthesis.

Consider the same scenario in a social studies course. Listing the causes of the American Civil War may be one way for students to demonstrate their knowledge. Such an assignment, though, does not give students an opportunity to practice the skills just mentioned. A teacher might alter such an assessment to require students to write legislation that addresses the problems of sectionalism, states' rights, and slavery in the 1850s. This idea upgrades the original assignment significantly, but the problem still has been provided for the students by the teacher. To make such an assignment real-life, the teacher shouldn't provide the problem but rather should have students identify the problem first and then solve the problem. Therefore, such an assignment might require students to write legislation in the 1850s or use government agencies to take steps to work proactively to head off the American Civil War. Such an assignment mirrors real life because students face a dilemma with no instructions on how to fix the problem. Students must draw on their comprehension of basic, fundamental concepts, and they must be able to understand the relationships between the fundamental concepts. Only then can they identify problems like sectionalism, states' rights questions, and slavery. Furthermore, students then must make connections, predict *if x then y*, and explain those cause and effect relationships. Once they have correctly identified the problem, they can set out to formulate solutions.

The second way a teacher can train students to successfully identify problems and then solve them is by helping students ask the right questions. This skill must be taught and developed over time. Students don't naturally ask the right questions, especially in an educational system that places so much emphasis on grades, testing, and performance. A great teacher knows that the difference between success and failure for students in identifying and solving problems may come down to asking the right questions. A great teacher constantly reminds students to ask questions and, more importantly, to ask the right questions. Furthermore, until students have grown adept at asking the right questions, a great teacher models this practice for her students often.

If a robotics class tackles a robot design project, for example, a great teacher must help team members ask the right questions so each will be in the best possible position for success. If the project requires robots to lift a ten pound dumbbell and then carry it a particular distance at a minimum speed, certain questions hold great value whereas others do not. For example, a teacher will not want to hear questions such as, "How do I get an A? How big does the robot need to be? When is the project due?" A great teacher will help students ask questions like, "How heavy is the object? What's the best way to grip or carry the object? How can we balance lifting strength with lightweight construction for a good combination of speed and strength?" instead. By not setting up the problem for the students and by guiding them toward asking the right questions, the teacher has empowered the students to identify the problem – creating a robot that can lift a heavy, awkwardly shaped object and carry it a minimum speed without tipping or stalling. Only once students have identified the problem can they successfully solve the problem. If these students identified the problem as making an A, making a three-foot-high robot, or making a robot that can travel faster than the other groups' robots, they likely would not have succeeded.

Just as history's greatest entrepreneurs, innovators, and inventors needed problem-solving skills, so too will the next generation of those professionals. Likewise, the next generation of doctors, engineers, teachers, programmers, electricians, business owners, and others will need problem-solving skills. The leaders in each of these fields and others, though, the game-changers, will be the ones who first can identify successfully the problems that need solving. If students do not receive training in this area in the athletic arena or in the classroom, where will they develop that skill? Students in the twenty-first century need great coaches and teachers alike to teach them to identify problems and create solutions, and students need as much work as possible in real-life situations as well as training in how to ask the right questions. Students will not develop these skills or receive training on their own. For such a crucial task, students need great teachers.

Section VII

Seek Continuous Improvement

1

The Personal Learning Network

> **"** I'm no innovator. If anything, I'm a stealer,
> or borrower. I've stolen or borrowed from **"**
> more people than you can shake a stick at.
>
> (Paul "Bear" Bryant, six-time NCAA national champion
> head football coach at the University of Alabama)

Legendary Princeton University men's basketball coach Pete Carril famously quoted his father when he said, "The strong take from the weak, but the smart take from the strong." When it comes to seeking continuous self-improvement, there hardly can be better advice. Smart coaches know to look to the most successful coaches and programs for ideas about how to improve their own coaching and their own programs. In the sports world, coaches know who the best coaches are and which programs have the most success year after year. The coaches who have built the most successful programs and have developed reputations as "the best" often entertain phone calls and email from around the country asking for advice, suggestions, plays, and strategies. Quite simply, Carril's father nailed it. The smart actively seek the strong in order to beg, borrow, or steal their ideas and plans in order to improve their own performance. But what about the strong? How do the best, most successful coaches continue to improve year after year? With so many aspiring and developing coaches seeking them out, how do the best in the business continue to maintain their competitive edge? They surround themselves with the rest of the best in the business.

Even the most successful coaches on the state, national, and international levels know they must continue to grow and improve if they are to maintain their competitive edge. To do so, many of the best coaches in the business have a network of other successful coaches with whom they communicate regularly. Conferences, books, videos, and the like work well as a means for coaches to learn some topics. However, for many coaches, learning from others far exceeds learning via books or conferences in terms of meaning and impact. Whether they realize it or not, highly successful coaches who lean on their peers and colleagues create for themselves what good teachers know as Personal Learning Networks. Personal Learning Networks (or PLNs) provide opportunities to collaborate, share advice, stay up to date on current trends and best practices, and find or offer support and leadership. Perhaps equally as important, PLNs provide opportunities to establish and foster relationships within the professional community.

Regarding the importance of PLNs for successful coaches, consider what some of the best coaches have to say. All-time winningest high school girls basketball coach *Leta Andrews* understands the importance of such networks. Andrews says, "Listen to the best. I have not coached with these coaches, but I have a very close relationship: Jody Conradt, Pat Summitt, John Wooden." *Brian Boland*, head coach of the 2012 NCAA national champion men's tennis team from the University of Virginia, echoes Andrews. Boland says when it comes to growing professionally, "I try to build relationships with as many people as I can."

Just as smart coaches do within the coaching world, smart teachers build their own PLNs within the world of education. As with continuous improvement in coaching, some things can't be learned in conferences or from a book in the same way they can be learned by interacting with peers or colleagues with more wisdom or life experience. Therein lies the power of networks like PLNs. PLNs, which truly could be described as professional social networking, enable educators to meet, stay in touch with, develop relationships with, and learn from other great educators literally around the world. By connecting with other educators, smart teachers can share ideas, solutions to problems or challenges, and suggestions for better teaching and learning. Through PLNs, smart teachers can connect with others in their specific academic discipline or grade level, or they can connect with teachers at large. Through PLNs, smart teachers can connect with other educators about technology, about new trends in education, about educational leadership, or practically anything. Furthermore, teachers who have ideas and expertise to offer the world can connect to others via PLNs to share their wisdom and experience.

Not too long ago, such communities of learners tended to be isolated to school buildings or districts. These communities of learners who exchanged ideas, pushed one another intellectually, and fostered a spirit of continuous improvement were known as professional learning communities, or PLCs. Now that technology has shrunk the world in ways no one would have believed or imagined only a generation ago, PLCs no longer have to be limited in size and scope. Indeed, PLCs have exploded onto the global scene in the form of PLNs. With the advancements in technology and the worldwide interest in establishing PLNs for teachers, a number of tools now exist online for facilitating PLNs. Some of the more popular PLN sites include ASCD Edge (ascdedge.ascd.org), Edmodo (www.edmodo.com), Classroom 2.0 (www.classroom20.com), and The Educator's PLN (edupln.ning.com). Even Facebook and LinkedIn offer educators a free and easy way to build professional relationships. All of these sites provide quick and easy ways for educators worldwide to connect with others and smart teachers worldwide use these daily.

In the last few years, one digital platform for creating PLNs has surpassed all others. While it may be surprising, Twitter quickly has become the number one PLN platform on the planet. Every day, the number of educators using Twitter grows, and many of these educators use Twitter as their PLN platform. Twitter provides a quick, easy, and free way to engage others around the world in conversation and to share information. Likewise, Twitter serves as a great tool to locate others who share similar interests. When Twitter users use the #, or hashtag, to tag or mark keywords or phrases, other users can search every tweet, or communication sent via Twitter, for keywords tagged accordingly. For example, a search on Twitter for #calculus or #edtech or #coachteach will yield countless conversations about those topics. Furthermore, educators who want to see what other education-related conversations are happening at any given time on Twitter can search online for education-related hashtags.

Peter Carril's father probably never imagined anything like personal learning networks in a digital world. Nevertheless, Mr. Carril gave his son sage advice when he said, "The smart take from the strong." For smart coaches and teachers, relationships with peers and colleagues provide tremendous opportunities for personal and professional continuous improvement. Regardless of how many years of experience they have or how much success they've enjoyed, coaches and teachers who want to continue to get better need to lean on others in their field who can offer advice, support, intellectual stimulation, or who simply can be a sounding board for ideas. Smart coaches and teachers don't have to steal from the strong; they simply need to take from the strong. Through PLNs, the wisdom of others is there for the taking for those smart enough to know where to look.

2

Read Voraciously

❝ I love to read . . . I have a stack of books so high it almost hits the ceiling. Those are the books I'm going to read before I die. I keep adding to them, so obviously that means I'll never catch up . . . **❞**

(*Anson Dorrance*, coach of 22 NCAA national championship women's soccer teams at the University of North Carolina and the NCAA all-time winningest women's soccer coach)

One of the most important and most meaningful ways to grow and improve as a coach or teacher happens to be one of the most affordable and fulfilling ways, too. Books! Conferences, clinics, seminars, personal learning networks, webinars, and other means of self-improvement certainly carry value. However, diving deep into a meaningful book can be more life-changing and enlightening than any conference or clinic. Some of the most successful people in the world read voraciously, and the same is true of some of the most successful coaches. These coaches are quick to credit much of their success to their interest in reading great books. Here are just a few examples:

- ◆ "Study and read . . ." (Leta Andrews)
- ◆ "I read books all the time on leadership, coaching, business and spirituality." (Patti Gerckens)

- ◆ "We read a lot of books about leadership and motivation." (Kenny Guillot)
- ◆ "I try to keep learning and studying. I read as many books as possible." (Dale Monsey)
- ◆ "I like to think outside of the box. I like to look at other disciplines to see how others approach problems and how they think. I talk with my colleagues, but I get more new ideas from reading in other areas and then looking for correlations." (Mick Haley)

The fact that great coaches read all the time speaks volumes about the value of reading and the value of being a life-long learner. One might be surprised to learn, though, that great coaches read far less about their sports than they do topics like leadership, motivation, management, psychology, team-building, business, mentorship, and the like. Great coaches often read outside the box, so to speak, and seek information and strategies that will help them become better leaders, managers, teachers, counselors, mentors, etc.

A great teacher, like great coaches, cherishes great books and understands the value of reading. There seem to be countless books available to teachers these days, which is great for teachers who read voraciously. Teachers of any content area can find scores of books specific to their content. Similarly, teachers easily can find dozens of books on pedagogical topics ranging from rigor to assessment to homework to technology integration to writing across the curriculum to creativity. A great teacher certainly has spent time throughout her career studying and reading not only in her content area but also in pedagogical areas in which she's interested. Such reading should never be abandoned. However, great coaches provide a stellar example for great teachers in terms of reading outside the realm of what might be expected. Books on leadership, management, coaching, mentorship, and more provide a wealth of information for great teachers who want to grow their skills in areas outside their content. With new books published daily, even the most voracious reader never will run short of books to read. The information and ideas are there for the taking.

The bottom line is that great teachers should seek continuous self-improvement within the pages of great books, whether those books are content related, pedagogical in nature, or related to leadership or similar topics. In the words of all-time winningest NCAA soccer coach Anson Dorrance, "I think that's the way to grow, to be curious about the world and everything that's in it, to find experts that have a better understanding in certain areas than you do and be motivated by them. I think that the ultimate way to improve yourself is by reading all the literature that's out there in the areas you're interested in."

3

See and Be Seen

> **"** We continue to grow professionally by attending
> clinics and also by hosting our own clinics;
> visiting teams that have similar offenses, defenses,
> and personnel; having college coaches come and
> talk to us about their philosophy; attending
> practices of other high schools and colleges;
> reading books about leadership and motivation. **"**
>
> (*Kenny Guillot*, four-time Louisiana state champion
> high school football coach)

When it comes to professional development, many coaches and teachers have valuable lessons to teach those with open minds and eager attitudes. Likewise, many eager coaches and teachers seek out wisdom and advice from peers, mentors, or others they respect in their respective fields. For a coach or teacher who wants to learn from someone else, reading a book or an article from that person might be an acceptable way to learn. Hearing that person speak, give a presentation, or do a presentation at a conference or seminar might be more powerful. Observing that person firsthand in his element, however, beats everything else, especially if there's an opportunity for dialogue between the observer and the observed. In terms of learning from peers and mentors, nothing beats the power of observation.

Great coaches have been practicing peer observation for decades. The veer offense from the game of football provides a powerful example of how peer observation can impact scores of coaches and programs over a very long period of time. In 1971, coach Jack Lengyel inherited the Marshall University football program after a tragic plane crash killed nearly all the coaches and players on the Marshall football team. Lengyel traveled to the campus of West Virginia where he spent three days observing and learning the veer offense from the gracious and accommodating Bobby Bowden (of eventual Florida State University fame). Bowden ran the offense at West Virginia but he didn't invent the veer. Bowden learned the offense from observing the University of Houston head football coach Bill Yeoman, the actual architect of the offense in the 1960s.

As teams who used the veer offense became more successful, more coaches wanted to install the offense with their own players. Especially in the days before VHS, DVDs, and the Internet, coaches' only sure-fire way to learn the veer was to load up the entire coaching staff and travel to a school willing to let the staff peek behind the curtain and observe every aspect of the veer teaching process. Coaches could watch game film of teams that used the veer offense. Coaches could study playbooks from other football programs. Eventually, coaches even could read books about the veer. However, nothing compared to observing coaching staff that taught the veer and taught it well. Why? Learning the veer offense and learning *how to teach* the veer offense were, and still are, vastly different.

Decades later, a number of the nation's perennially successful collegiate and high school programs – including the Air Force Academy, Georgia Tech, De La Salle High School in California, and John Curtis High School in Louisiana – still run the veer offense or a variation of the offense. Every year, coaches from around the nation travel to see the coaches from these schools in action and to observe veer offense instruction. In today's digital world, reading about or watching video of the veer offense is quick and easy, but making the veer offense successful requires more than watching the offense or reading about it.

Making the veer offense successful requires an understanding of how to teach the offense, and that requires observation.

Peer observation can be as powerful for classroom teachers as it can be for coaches. Though any teacher can learn from peer observation, for new or inexperienced teachers in particular, this practice can be quite powerful. In recent years, the educational system in Finland has burst onto the international education scene and has developed a reputation as one of the world's most effective systems. Thanks in part to books like *Finnish Lessons: What Can the World Learn from Educational Change in Finland?* by Pasi Sahlberg, the documentary film *The Finland Phenomenon* by Tony Wagner, and other media exposure, the world has been able to see some of what makes Finland's education system work so well. Part of what the world has discovered about Finland's success is that Finnish teacher education programs rely heavily on teacher trainees and new teachers spending a significant amount of time immersed in the observation process, both observing master teachers and one another, and being observed. To be effective, though, peer observation must be executed properly.

A wise coach or teacher understands that observation entails far more than simply seeing or watching. Peer observation goes far deeper than sitting on a field or in a classroom watching another teacher. The website of the Center for Teaching and Learning (located at the University of Texas at Austin) describes peer observation as involving "faculty peers who review an instructor's performance through classroom observation and examination of instructional materials including course design." The website goes on to say that peer observation should include "reviewing the teaching process" and its "relationship to learning." Finnish teacher education programs, along with the best in the United States and elsewhere in the world, place great emphasis on this very intentional process of reviewing the teaching process and its relationship to learning.

When done correctly, peer observation involves carefully watching what a teacher teaches, how she teaches, and to what extent the students are engaged and learning. Peer observation involves looking for both verbal and nonverbal communication from teacher and students. Additionally, a good peer observation process involves post-observation dialogue either between the observer and the observed or between multiple observers. In order for an observer to get the most out of observation, a rubric, checklist, or other instrument for assessment of best classroom practices can be a powerful tool to use during the observation. Many school districts or building administrators have teacher assessment tools that should be available for teachers to use during peer observations. For teachers who do not have access to such peer observation guides, a quick search online for "peer observation rubric," "classroom observation instrument," or "classroom observation guide" should produce myriad downloadable and printable documents that can be used to guide peer observations. Such an instrument, once completed, can serve as a great roadmap for post-observation dialogue. If the observer asks good questions of the observed after the lesson – Why did you pause so long after asking your questions? How did you know you needed to repeat that concept? How were you able to gauge the number of students who still were confused? Where did you learn the strategy for breaking that difficult concept down into these simpler parts? – the observer can glean valuable insight into what made the teaching so effective.

Through honest and meaningful dialogue, the observer will not be the only peer observation participant to learn and get better. With good post-observation dialogue, which must be transparent and non-threatening, the observed can hear from the observer good feedback that can improve his pedagogy, too. The observer can tell the observed teacher, "I understand the main point of the lesson to be . . ., was that your intention?" "I understood you to say . . ., is that accurate?" "I noticed you called on boys more often than girls," and so on. Such feedback can help the observed teacher reflect on the lesson she just taught and perhaps identify ways to fine-tune the process. The observer also can provide meaningful feedback in the form of questions like, "What if you did this or that differently?" or "Have you ever considered trying that concept using peer tutoring or collaboration?"

In terms of professional growth opportunities, peer observation offers perhaps the greatest bang for the buck. A coach or teacher could, of course, travel across the country or around the world to observe great teaching, at considerable expense. In truth, though, great teaching may be happening across the hall, across campus, or just across town. Someone seeking peer observation opportunities probably should start locally, either on campus or within the district, and then branch out to other schools. Compared with the cost of attending conferences or seminars, the cost of a substitute teacher for a day could pay significant dividends if a teacher returns from classroom visits energized, renewed, challenged, and ready to implement some new and effective teaching techniques.

When seeking peers to observe, teachers often seek colleagues who teach the same grade and the same subject area. Peer observation involving such similar teachers can be a powerful practice in terms of fine-tuning one's approach to teaching a particular concept, grade, or content area. However, great teaching is great teaching, regardless of the content area or the age of the learner. Therefore, peer observation can be a powerful practice for coaches and teachers who step outside their comfort zone. A basketball coach can learn from a good volleyball coach just as a softball coach can learn from a good football coach. A calculus teacher can learn a great deal from a third-grade teacher coaching her students through multiplication and division. A fourth-grade English teacher can learn much from an Advanced Placement Language and Composition teacher. A Chinese teacher can learn from a Spanish teacher. The list goes on and on because great teaching is great teaching, regardless of if the learning occurs on a court or field or in a lab or classroom. Wise coaches and teachers committed to self-improvement seek out great teaching so they can observe, learn, and continue to improve.

4

The Power of Video

❝ I also use video analysis to assess my
own performance in matches,
how I might make adjustments. **❞**

(*Sean Fleming*, head coach of Canada
Soccer's U-17 men's national team)

Although athletic competitions last anywhere from one to three hours, the action often occurs at lightning speed. Even the most astute observer will miss something during the course of the game. Entire coaching staffs from both teams watch and pay attention, but things still go unnoticed in the heat of the moment. During an athletic competition, there simply are too many things happening at once for even the best coach to process as the saga unfolds. Therein lies the power of the video recording.

Students of the game remember legendary Andover football coach Steve Sorota, who coached Andover from 1938 to 1978, as one of the early pioneers of the study of game film. Technology has come a long way since the days of the clunky reel-to-reel cameras like Sorota may have used. Digital recording capability now makes it possible to record practically anything anywhere at any time, and very inexpensively. Using anything from GoPro to Flip to smartphones to dual-purpose cameras like the Canon 5D to high-end video cameras like the Sony HDR-CX580, coaches can record games, practices, and even one-on-one workout sessions easily and on any budget.

Just as recording technology has advanced incredibly since the days of reel-to-reel cameras, video viewing has progressed quite a bit from the days of the black-and-white reel-to-reel projectors with no audio. Video now can be played directly from recording devices, from files archived on computers, from files stored on smartphones and tablets, and even streamed anywhere in the world from the cloud. Any coach or player can view video from anywhere using a smartphone, tablet, computer, or TV.

As if the advances in video recording and viewing aren't enough, coaches and players can edit video more quickly and easily than ever before with no expensive software needed. Using online services like Hudl, coaches can edit video to meet the needs of their own staff and players as well as for other coaches (as in sports like football where coaches must exchange game film). Gone are the days of copying VHS tapes and even DVDs. Players can create their own highlight films now for recruitment purposes, too, instead of relying on videocassettes and DVDs. Interestingly, even though coaches use digital recording devices instead of actual film for recording, game video and highlight videos often are still referred to as game film or highlight film.

To say that video has revolutionized the sports world and the way coaches teach would be a gross understatement. As mentioned earlier, too many things happen in the course of a game or match for the coaches and players to see or remember everything. By recording games, especially from multiple angles, coaches can scrutinize every imaginable aspect of a team's (or opponent's) performance. Many of the most successful coaches in the sports world, regardless of the sport or level of competition, spend a great deal of time analyzing and breaking down game film. From studying game film, a good coach can identify a team's strengths, weaknesses, tendencies, and areas that need improvement. By painstakingly grading game film, or quantifying a team's performance, a good coach can use the film as a powerful teaching tool with the team.

The same goes for practices. Brian Boland, men's tennis coach at the University of Virginia, led his team to the NCAA national championship in 2013 thanks in part to the use of video. Boland says, "One of the best tools we use at the University of Virginia is video. Filming a player's match or practice is such a great way to provide proof to a player regarding what he needs to improve or what he is doing better. We use video as often as we can and I would recommend it to any coach out there." Boland certainly holds good company in assessment of video as a tool. Legendary and all-time winningest high school girls basketball coach Leta Andrews concurs. Says Andrews, video "is an aid to me to analyze games and practice sessions. The athletes can see where they need to improve." By recording practices or one-on-one practice sessions and showing the video to the player or players, a good coach can provide indisputable evidence players can use to correct mistakes and get better or to continue doing a particular thing well.

For teachers who are willing to take an honest look at themselves and their teaching, video can be as transformational in the classroom as it has been for coaches in the sports world. By using a video recording of a classroom while teaching, a teacher can get an accurate account of what's actually happening in terms of both teaching and learning. This simple and inexpensive process can be accomplished using any number of simple recording devices and should not be cost prohibitive. If a teacher has difficulty or needs help with the process, the school technology department usually will be delighted to help. If a classroom lacks a great vantage point for a single camera to capture everything, using a second camera from a different location and angle can be valuable.

The idea of being recorded may be an intimidating thought for some teachers, but a good teacher who really wants to improve should consider this as a self-assessment tool. Even Canada Soccer's U-17 men's national coach uses video as a way to support his self-improvement. In addition to other professional growth activities, Sean Fleming says, "I also use video analysis to assess my own performance in matches, how I might make adjustments." Fleming, a former teacher and great teaching coach, models exactly the attitude a good teacher needs when considering the use of recorded class sessions as a way to find areas of both strength and future growth.

As in an athletic competition, too much action occurs during any given class for a teacher to observe and process it all. Using video to record a class session can reveal myriad things even a good teacher might never notice otherwise. After watching a recorded class session, a good teacher might say, "Do I always stand mostly on the right side of the room? Do I always call on the boys more often than the girls? Do I always answer my own questions instead of waiting a little longer for the students to answer? Does Sarah always lift her hand only halfway when she has a question? How often does Johnny have his cell phone hidden behind his book, and is it any wonder Johnny rarely understands my instructions the first time? Do the students always glance repeatedly at the clock on the wall while I'm teaching?"

To make the most of the experience, a good teacher watches the playback objectively and critically. Taking notes and jotting down observations of one's teaching often makes for an enlightening experience. For a teacher who may not know where to begin in terms of critiquing her own teaching and classroom environment, she may want to ask an administrator for a sample observation rubric or other assessment or evaluation tool. Additionally, inviting a trusted colleague or mentor to watch the video and offer feedback can be a valuable exercise. Many of the most successful coaches around use video to evaluate not only their teams but also themselves. Why would a good teacher not learn from the best and give this simple but powerful exercise a try right away?

5

The Game Has Changed . . .

> ❝Athletes and people are happiest when they are improving . . . You are either getting better or you are getting worse . . . I find it really tough at any level, but especially with an Olympian that's no longer getting any better and not improving . . . we have to deal with some tough stuff. We do whatever we can – with technology, with feedback, with multiple coaches coming from different angles – to keep them improving, because that's when they are performing at their best. ❞
>
> (*Marv Dunphy*, member of the Volleyball Hall of Fame, five-time NCAA national champion as head coach of Pepperdine University men's volleyball team, and gold medal winner as head coach of the 1988 Olympic team)

The game has changed. What game, you ask? Well, virtually every game in the modern sports world has changed since its inception. For some sports, rules have changed, gameplay has changed, equipment has changed, scoring has changed, and even the length of the season has changed. The three-point line in basketball, the designated hitter in baseball, and the forward pass in football each have irreversibly changed their respective sports. For other sports, the players today are bigger, stronger, and faster than ever before, and the very nature of those particular sports has been forever altered because of the changes in the athletes. Usain Bolt in track and field, Lionel Messi in soccer, Tiger Woods in golf, Michael Phelps in swimming, and Kareem Abdul-Jabbar and Brittney Griner in basketball have elevated the level of "excellence" to new heights in their respective sports. Additionally, many nuances of the major sports have changed.

To be successful in the sports world today, a good coach must understand change. He not only must acknowledge that his sport changes but also must take measures to keep up with the changes. He must be willing to change his practice approach and his game plan. He must be willing to approach players differently. He must be willing to approach every aspect of the game differently. If there is a coach today using the same approach, same game plan, and same practice plan he did 20 years ago, chances are that his program ranks somewhere other than at the top. Because rules, equipment, scoring, and even players have changed through the years, no good coach would stubbornly resist change and refuse to stay current. Imagine a basketball coach running the same plays he used before the introduction of the three-point line.

A good coach works hard to stay on top of how his particular sport continues to change or he simply gets passed by. An NCAA or National Football League defensive coordinator had better put in extra time to understand how the New Orleans Saints and the Baylor Bears, engineered by Sean Payton and Art Briles, respectively, have changed the game of football offensively. A National Hockey League coach had better work hard to find a way to approach Ken Hitchcock's frustrating, defense-first style of hockey. Coaches who do not keep up with other programs' innovations will become obsolete very quickly.

As with the world of sports, the world of education has changed. Historically, education has changed very little until very recently. The stand-and-deliver model of teaching by lecture dominated education for centuries, dating back to the advent of universities hundreds of years ago. Even late into the twentieth century and beyond, such obsolete pedagogy has managed to hang on for dear life in some schools even though the world outside the classroom walls has been changing at an incredible rate. In recent years, however, the rules of education have changed, the art of teaching has changed, scoring and assessment have changed, the lengths of the days and years have changed, and even the students have changed. Imagine a teacher teaching science the way she taught it in the 1970s, or history, or art. Inconceivable! For a good teacher, these changes present opportunities to change with the times and explore new and exciting best practices.

A good teacher understands that both teaching and learning have changed. Whereas classrooms once were cutting edge with one Apple IIe for students to share, many classrooms today have tablets or laptops in every student's hands. Classrooms of days gone by used sticks of chalk with chalk boards or blackboards, while today's classrooms often boast interactive whiteboards. Blended classes, digital textbooks, state standardized testing, increasingly competitive college admissions, scores of proprietary curriculum choices, Advanced Placement courses, and more, have changed not only what teachers teach but how they teach. Similarly, what students learn and how they learn have changed. Research has shown repeatedly that the one-size-fits-all assembly-line method of educating students used so much throughout the twentieth century leads to disinterest and disengagement with twenty-first-century kids.

A good teacher recognizes that today's students differ even from students ten years ago. Today's students are more plugged in than ever. Today's students have different life goals than students a generation ago. Today's students face a future that is more uncertain than ever before and employment statistics that are far from encouraging. As a result, what students need in the classroom varies greatly from what students needed in past generations. A good teacher changes her game plan, or lesson plans, to accommodate these changing needs. Because students' needs have changed and because the ways students' learn best have changed, a good teacher stays current on changes in teaching and learning by reading, researching, observing others, and experimenting with new approaches.

A good teacher, unafraid to change with the times, rewrites his game plan as often as necessary in order to stay current with best practices. In terms of teaching quality, experience can be priceless. As recent research shows, however, there exists no direct correlation between teacher experience and teacher effectiveness. This largely results from career educators' inability or desire not to change and update their game plans to give today's students what they need. The best teacher in any given building may or may not be the most experienced teacher. The best teacher in the building, though, will not be the one using the same yellowed notes he used three decades ago. The best teacher in the building will not be the one using the same exams he used back when mimeograph machines with purple toner were all the rage. The best teacher in the building will not be the one who has memorized all the lectures and can deliver them with no notes or outlines in front of him. As with coaches who hold on too long to the old ways of doing things, quite possibly, the game of teaching has passed some of these teachers by, thus rendering them obsolete in the twenty-first-century classroom. The best teacher in the building, regardless of years of experience, does what all good teachers do: he evaluates his game plan often and rewrites his game plan as often as necessary to accommodate the changing needs of the students and the changing landscape of the real world and does not cling to obsolete pedagogies.

Perhaps baseball coach *John Cohen* of Mississippi State University sums this up best. Having led his Bulldogs to not only the College World Series finals in 2013 but also to the most wins in program history in a season, Cohen understands that change and evolution are crucial to continued success. He says of his own coaching and teaching journey, "the six most dangerous words in the English language: We've always done it this way. That's dangerous because the world is changing. If we were doing it the same way that I was doing it as a young coach 20 years ago, we'd be doing the program a huge disservice. It's a challenge to make sure you're constantly evolving." As Cohen will testify, the challenge certainly is worth it, for you and for those you teach.

Keeping in mind that the game has changed, and will continue to change, the obvious question is, "Will you?"

AFTERWORD

Like so many great coaches and teachers, *Cori Close*, women's basketball coach at UCLA, attributes her commitment to teaching to two teachers who changed her life forever: her father, a teacher and coach of more than 30 years, and the incomparable John Wooden. These two men, each in his own way, affected Close and gave direction to her life as an educator. Of her experiences with these two men, Cori Close reflects that they "really taught me that it's all the same thing (coaching and teaching)." Says Close of her father, "My dad was a teacher . . . a lot of what I've done in coaching is based on watching him teach for many, many years." Regarding Wooden, Close tells a powerful story of an encounter she had once with one of Wooden's former players, who moved her to tears with testimony of how he was impacted, molded, and empowered by Wooden's teaching. She says, "I thought to myself right then and there, my third or fourth day on the job, I wanted our players to talk like that: 'I'm having opportunities because of what women's basketball taught me at UCLA.'" From that day in 1995 until Wooden's passing, Close forged and maintained a relationship with Wooden and soaked in like a sponge his wisdom on basketball, teaching, and life.

To pay it forward, Close now teaches and mentors both current and former players so they can be impacted and, in turn, impact others. "We choose to be lifestyle givers and not lifestyle takers. It was just seamless in all the people I was around," she says. She recalls a recent incident with one of her former players who has committed her own life to coaching and teaching. "I was with a ball player of mine who's now in coaching and she's going through some rough stuff, and saying, 'Do I want to do this? I'm in a really successful program and we're winning a lot of games, but I just don't know if I want to do it if it can't be transformational like it was in my life.' And I thought, you know, that's what it is: life lessons. The average Division I basketball player spends over 3500 hours in her sport over four years, and only 4 percent of those hours are in games. I better be doing something with the other 96 percent. The reality is, if the only thing I ever give a young lady is a better jump shot, even a WNBA career, even a banner at Pauley Pavilion . . . It's empty without her having a transformational experience. Because it [teaching] has affected me and my life's been changed by it [teaching], there's no other choice but to pay it forward the same way."

Coach Cori Close gets it. "Basketball is my classroom," she says, "but it's really about 'How do I reach that student?' 'How do I make something more relevant to her?' Whether or not I'm teaching in front of a group . . . or whether I'm finding ways to reach my team, I think coaching and teaching are synonymous."

Whether its basketball or reading or calculus that you teach in your classroom, my hope for you while you are on your own teaching journey is that you will become for your students what her father and John Wooden were to Cori Close and what Cori Close has committed to being for her players: an impactful, game-changing teacher committed to making your teaching a transformational experience for your students.

Lightning Source UK Ltd.
Milton Keynes UK
UKHW02f2018190618
324487UK00016B/383/P